Super Cheap Venice Travel Guide

Redefining Super Cheap	10
How to Enjoy ALLOCATING Money in Venice	20
How to feel RICH in Venice	23
Priceline Hack to get a Luxury Hotel on the Cheap	30
Hotels with frequent last-minute booking discounts:	31
Cheapest Guesthouses in Venice	37
How to use this book	48
OUR SUPER CHEAP TIPS…	49
How to Find Super Cheap Flights to Venice	49
How to Find CHEAP FIRST-CLASS Flights to Venice	53
Go Book Shopping	87
RECAP: How to enjoy a $5,000 trip to Venice for $300	100
Money Mistakes in Venice	105
The secret to saving HUGE amounts of money when travelling to Venice is…	106
Thank you for reading	110
Bonus Travel Hacks	114
Common pitfalls when it comes to allocating money to your desires while traveling	115
Hack your allocations for your Venice Trip	118

MORE TIPS TO FIND CHEAP FLIGHTS	121
What Credit Card Gives The Best Air Miles?	126
Frequent Flyer Memberships	130
How to get 70% off a Cruise	132
Pack like a Pro	133
Relaxing at the Airport	136
Money: How to make it, spend it and save it while travelling	138
How to earn money WHILE travelling	139
How to spend money	142
How to save money while travelling	147
Travel Apps That'll Make Budget Travel Easier	148
How NOT to be ripped off	150
Small tweaks on the road add up to big differences in your bank balance	156
Where and How to Make Friends	159
When unpleasantries come your way…	160
Hacks for Families	171
Safety	174
How I got hooked on budget travelling	177
A final word…	179
Our Writers	180
Copyright	182

"Venice is the city of mirrors, the city of mirages, at once solid and liquid, at once air and stone." Erica Jon.

The Magical Power of Bargains

Have you ever felt the rush of getting a bargain? And then found good fortune just keeps following you?

Let me give you an example. In 2009, I graduated into the worst global recession for generations. One unemployed day, I saw a suit I knew I could get a job in. The suit was £250. Money I didn't have. Imagine my shock when the next day I saw the exact same suit (in my size) in the window of a second-hand shop (thrift store) for £18! I bought the suit and after three months of interviewing, without a single call back, within a week of owning that £18 suit, I was hired on a salary far above my expectations. That's the powerful psychological effect of getting an incredible deal. It builds a sense of excitement and happiness that literally creates miracles.

I have no doubt that Venice's winding waterways, ornate bridges, and stunning architecture will uplift and inspire you but when you add the bargains from this book to your vacation, not only will you save a ton of money; you are guaranteed to enjoy a truly magical trip to Venice.

Who this book is for and why anyone can enjoy budget travel

Did you know you can fly on a private jet for $500? Yes, a fully private jet. Complete with flutes of champagne and reclinable creamy leather seats. Your average billionaire spends $20,000 on the exact same flight. You can get it for $500 when you book private jet empty leg flights. This is just one of thousands of ways you can travel luxuriously on a budget. You see there is a big difference between being cheap and frugal.

When our brain hears the word "budget" it hears deprivation, suffering, agony, even depression. But budget travel need not be synonymous with hostels and pack lunches. You can enjoy an incredible and luxurious trip to Venice on a budget, just like you can enjoy a private jet flight for 10% of the normal cost when you know how.

Over 20 years of travel has taught me I could have a 20 cent experience that will stir my soul more than a $100 one. Of course, sometimes the reverse is true, my point is, spending money on travel is the best investment you can make but it doesn't have to be at levels set by hotels and attractions with massive ad spends and influencers who are paid small fortunes to get you to buy into something you could have for a fraction of the cost.

This book is for those who love bargains and want to have the cold hard budget busting facts to hand (which is why we've included so many one page charts, which you can use as a quick reference), but otherwise, the book provides plenty of tips to help you shape your own Venice experience.

We have designed these travel guides to give you a unique planning tool to experience an unforgettable trip without spending the ascribed tourist budget.

This guide focuses on Venice's unbelievable bargains. Of course, there is little value in traveling to Venice and not experiencing everything it has to offer. Where possible, we've included super cheap workarounds or listed the experience in the Loved but Costly section.

When it comes to luxury budget travel, it's all about what you know. You can have all the feels without most of the bills. A few days spent planning can save you thousands. Luckily, we've done the planning for you, so you can distill the information in minutes not days, leaving you to focus on what matters: immersing yourself in the sights, sounds and smells of Venice, meeting awesome new people and feeling relaxed and happy.

This book reads like a good friend has travelled the length and breadth of Venice and brought you back incredible insider tips.

So, grab a cup of tea or coffee, put your feet up and relax; you're about to enter the world of enjoying Venice on the Super Cheap. Oh, and don't forget a biscuit. You need energy to plan a trip of a lifetime on a budget.

GET A BARGAIN RIGHT NOW

Sign-up to our newsletter. They are never annoying because we ONLY EVER send links to our books when they are FREE.
supercheapinsiderguides.com

(Our bestsellers include bucket-list destinations like Maldives, Bora Bora and Paris)

Super Cheap Venice is <u>not</u> for travellers with the following needs:

1. You require a book with detailed offline travel maps. Super Cheap Insider Guides are best used with Google Maps - download before you travel to make the most of your time and money.
2. You would like thousands of accommodation, food and attraction recommendations; by definition, cheapest is often singular. We only include maximum value recommendations. We purposively leave out over-priced attractions when there is no workaround.
3. You would like detailed write-ups about hotels/Airbnbs/Restaurants. We are bargain hunters first and foremost. We dedicate our time to finding the best deals, not writing flowery language about their interiors. Plus, things change. If I had a pound for every time I'd read a Lonely Planet description only to find the place totally different, I would be a rich man. Always look at online reviews for the latest up-to-date information.

If you want to save A LOT of money while comfortably enjoying an unforgettable trip to Venice, minus the marketing, hype, scams and tourist traps read on.

Redefining Super Cheap

The value you get out of Super Cheap Venice is not based on what you paid for it; it's based on what you do with it. You can only do great things with it if you believe saving money is worth your time. Charging things to your credit card and thinking 'oh I'll pay it off when I get home' is something you won't be tempted to do if you change your beliefs now. Think about what you associate with the word cheap, because you make your beliefs and your beliefs make you.

I grew up thinking you had to spend more than you could afford to have a good time traveling. Now I've visited 190 countries, I know nothing is further from the truth. Before you embark upon reading our specific tips for Venice think about your associations with the word cheap.

Here are the dictionary definitions of cheap:

- Costing very little; relatively low in price; inexpensive: a cheap dress.
- costing little labor or trouble: Words are cheap.
- charging low prices: a very cheap store.
- Of little account; of small value; mean; shoddy: Cheap conduct; cheap workmanship.
- Embarrassed; sheepish: He felt cheap about his mistake.
- Stingy; miserly:
  He's too cheap to buy his own brother a cup of coffee.

Three out of six definitions have extremely negative connotations. The 'super cheap' we're talking about in this book is not shoddy, embarrassed, or stingy.
We added the super to reinforce our message. Super's dictionary definition stands for 'a super quality'. Super Cheap stands for enjoying the best on the lowest budget. Question other people's definitions of cheap so you're not blinded to possibilities, poten-

tial, and prosperity. Here are some new associations to consider forging:

Shoddy

Cheap stuff doesn't last is an adage marketing companies have drilled into consumers. However, by asking vendors the right questions cheap doesn't mean something won't last. I had a $10 backpack last for 8 years and a $100 suitcase bust on the first journey.

A study out of San Francisco University found that people who spent money on experiences rather than things were happier. Memories last forever, not things, even expensive things. And as we will show you during this guide, you don't need to pay to create glorious memories.[1]

Embarrassed

I have friends who routinely pay more to vendors because they think their money is putting food on this person's table. Paradoxically, Cuban doctors are driving taxis because they earn more money; it's not always a good thing for the place you're visiting to pay more and can cause unwanted distortion in their culture - Airbnb pushing out renters is an obvious example. Think carefully about whether the extra money is helping people or incentivising greed.

Stingy

Cheap can be eco-friendly. Buying thrift clothes is cheap, but you also help the Earth. Many travellers are often disillusioned by the reality of traveling since the places on our bucket-lists are overcrowded. Cheap can take you away from the crowds. You can find balance and harmony being cheap. "Remember a journey is

---

[1] Paulina Pchelin & Ryan T. Howell (2014) The hidden cost of value-seeking: People do not accurately forecast the economic benefits of experiential purchases, The Journal of Positive Psychology, 9:4, 322-334, DOI: 10.1080/17439760.2014.898316

best measured in friends, rather than miles." – Tim Cahill. And making friends is free!

A recent survey by Credit Karma found 50% of Millennials and Gen Z get into debt traveling. **Please don't allow credit card debt to be an unwanted souvenir you take home.** As you will see from this book, there's so much you can enjoy in Venice for free, some many unique bargains and so many ways to save money! You just need to want to!

Discover Venice

The city built on a lagoon is simply incomparable. Venice is 117 small islands connected by 400 bridges and 50 canals; dazzling sights, museums and mouth-watering restaurants. The city dates back to 421. In the late 13th century Venice was the most prosperous city in Europe. Today it's a mecca for millions of tourists who want to bathe their senses in the ancient architecture and stunning blue hues of its canals. The first time you see Venice, you know miracles are possible. There is a city built on water. Its historic beauty is best experienced on foot. Though you must ride down the Grand Canal on a Varapetto to enjoy the aesthetic game of "I have more money than you do" Still just walking through the streets is an amazing experience where you will feel like your being transported back in time surrounded by crumbling walls and architecture. Marvel as the gondolier navigate the arches of Venetian bridges - which were built just high enough to allow a them to pass.

Although it is a beauty, it is riddled with many tourist traps, 5€ soft drinks and €10 coffee! The key to keeping it cheap is to get off the tourist track and find the local deals. If you follow the advice in this guide you could definitely get away with having the time of your life on about $50 a day per person including luxury accommodation in Venice.

Some of Venice's Best Bargains

Save time and money at St Mark's Basilica

Before visiting St Mark's Basilica buy an online voucher for timed entrance to avoid the long lines for just 1.5 Euros: http:// www.venetoinside.com/en/saint_mark_s_basilica/

Enjoy Cicchetti

Cicchetti is a Venetian cuisine that consists of small, appetizers, similar to Spanish tapas or Italian antipasti. It is typically enjoyed as a pre-dinner snack between 5:00 pm and 8:00 pm. Most bars charge a small fee for each snack but its usually under 2 euros.. Here are some must-try cicchetti bars in Venice:

1. Al Timon: Located in the Cannaregio district, Al Timon is a popular cicchetti bar that offers a range of delicious appetizers, including crostini, fried fish, and meatballs. The bar has a lovely outdoor seating area overlooking the canal.
2. Cantina do Mori: Established in 1462, Cantina do Mori is one of the oldest cicchetti bars in Venice. The bar has a cozy, historic ambiance and serves a variety of appetizers, including pickled vegetables, meats, and cheeses.
3. All'Arco: This small, unassuming cicchetti bar is located near the Rialto Bridge and is known for its fresh, high-quality ingredients. The bar offers a range of appetizers, including fried seafood, meats, and vegetables.
4. Osteria Bancogiro: Located near the Grand Canal, Osteria Bancogiro is a popular spot for cicchetti and wine. The bar offers a range of appetizers, including fried fish, meats, and cheeses.
5. Cantine del Vino già Schiavi: This lively cicchetti bar is located in the Dorsoduro district and is known for its extensive wine selection and delicious appetizers.

Pro tip: during the annual Festa del Redentore celebration in July, many local restaurants and bars offer free cicchetti to visitors. Similarly, during the annual Festa della Sensa celebration in May, your find lots of free Cicchetti.

Dine on delicious pizza for €6

When you're out and about exploring Venice, it can be difficult to know where to eat. Like with most tourist overrun areas, restaurants are overpriced and underwhelming. Thankfully this is not the case with Al Bacco Felice (Address: 94; Calle dei Amai) Pizzas start at just €6!

Enjoy a mini gondola ride for a fraction of the regular price

Find a Traghetto (details on page 58) for crossing the grand canal. It's a mini gondola ride for two euros!

Indulge in a Venetian set lunch

Osteria Mocenigo offers an amazingly good value set lunches which include pasta, salad, wine and coffee for just €12!

How to Enjoy ALLO-CATING Money in Venice

'Money's greatest intrinsic value—and this can't be overstated—is its ability to give you control over your time.' - Morgan Housel

Notice I have titled the chapter how to enjoy allocating money in Venice. I'll use saving and allocating interchangeably in the book, but since most people associate saving to feel like a turtleneck, that's too tight, I've chosen to use wealth language. Rich people don't save. They allocate. What's the difference? Saving can feel like something you don't want or wish to do and allocating has your personal will attached to it.

And on that note, it would be helpful if you considered removing the following words and phrase from your vocabulary for planning and enjoying your Venice trip:

- Wish
- Want
- Maybe someday

These words are part of poverty language. Language is a dominant source of creation. Use it to your advantage. You don't have to wish, want or say maybe someday to Venice. You can enjoy the same things millionaires enjoy in Venice without the huge spend.

'People don't like to be sold-but they love to buy.' - Jeffrey Gitomer.

Every good salesperson who understands the quote above places obstacles in the way of their clients' buying. Companies create waiting lists, restaurants pay people to queue outside in order to create demand. People reason if something is so in demand, it must be worth having but that's often just marketing. Take this sales maxim 'People don't like to be sold-but they love to buy and flip it on its head to allocate your money in Venice on things YOU desire. You love to spend and hate to be sold. That means when something comes your way, it's not 'I can't afford it,' it's 'I don't want it' or maybe 'I don't want it right now'.

Saving money doesn't mean never buying a latte, never taking a taxi, never taking vacations (of course, you bought this book). Only you get to decide on how you spend and on what. Not an advice columnist who thinks you can buy a house if you never eat avocado toast again.

I love what Kate Northrup says about affording something: "If you really wanted it you would figure out a way to get it. If it were that VALUABLE to you, you would make it happen."

I believe if you master the art of allocating money to bargains, it can feel even better than spending it! Bold claim, I know. But here's the truth: Money gives you freedom and options. The more you keep in your account and or invested the more freedom and options you'll have. The principal reason you should save and allocate money is TO BE FREE! Remember, a trip's main purpose is relaxation, rest and enjoyment, aka to feel free.

When you talk to most people about saving money on vacation. They grimace. How awful they proclaim not to go wild on your vacation. If you can't get into a ton of debt enjoying your once-in-a-lifetime vacation, when can you?

When you spend money 'theres's a sudden rush of dopamine which vanishes once the transaction is complete. What happens in the brain when you save money? It increases feelings of security and peace. You don't need to stress life's uncertainties. And having a greater sense of peace can actually help you save more money.' Stressed out people make impulsive financial choices, calm people don't.'

The secret to enjoying saving money on vacation is very simple: never save money from a position of lack. Don't think 'I wish I could afford that'. Choose not to be marketed to. Choose not to consume at a price others set. Don't save money from the flawed premise you don't have enough. Don't waste your time living in the box that society has created, which says saving money on vacation means sacrifice. It doesn't.

Traveling to Venice can be an expensive endeavor if you don't approach it with a plan, but you have this book which is packed with tips. The biggest other asset is your perspective.

How to feel RICH in Venice

You don't need millions in your bank to **feel rich**. Feeling rich feels different to every person.

"Researchers have pooled data on the relationship between money and emotions from more than 1.6 million people across 162 countries and found that **wealthier people feel more positive "self-regard emotions" such as confidence, pride and determination.**"

Here are things to see, do and taste in Venice, that will have you overflowing with gratitude for your luxury trip to Venice.

- You can snag a grand canal view and a 10 euro pizza at Riva Rialto.
- While money can't buy happiness, it can buy cake and isn't that sort of the same thing? Jokes aside, Mamafè - Salento Bakery in Venice have turned cakes and pastries into edible art. Visit to taste the most delicious croissant in Venice.
- While Caffé Florian (est 1720) is considered one of the oldest cafes in the world its prices are commiserate with its experience and beauty. For a cheaper but still cute option head to Torrefazione Cannaregio - Speciality Coffee.
- While you might not be staying in a penthouse, you can still enjoy the same views. Visit rooftop bars in Venice, like Skyline Rooftop Bar to enjoy incredible sunset views for the price of just one drink. And if you want to continue enjoying libations, head over to Bacareto da Lele for a dirt-cheap happy hour, lots of reasonably priced (and delicious) cocktails and cheap delicious snacks.

Those are just some ideas for you to know that visiting Venice on a budget doesn't have to feel like sacrifice or constriction. Now let's get into the nuts and bolts of Venice on the super cheap.

Planning your trip

When to visit
The first step in saving money on your Venice trip is timing. Avoid peak season - June, July and August where hotel rooms and flights will triple. If you are not tied to school holidays, the best time to visit is during the shoulder-season months. September to November when tourists desert the city, meaning lowered hotel rates and barren canals but don't despair there are bargains all your round but when you visit will determine the luxury level of your accommodation. If staying in a five-star hotel is a must for you in Venice, then arrange your visit for the low season or shoulder months.

Where to stay?
Stay on Giudecca, a 5 minute ride via vaporetto (water bus) from St Mark's Square. It's the cheapest island within close proximity to the attractions. Marco's (our local in Venice) family have lived on Giudecca for 15 years and consider it to be very safe. That's apparently one reason its popular with young professionals too.

The cheapest place to stay
If you're travelling solo hostels are your best option, both for meeting people and saving pennies. Hostels on the islands start at $15. If you want more privacy, you can get an airbnb near Messer (the train station) they are cheaper. I met many travellers who stayed at The Generator Hostel and spoke very highly of it.

It's a design hostel, put the biggest plus is that the kitchen has authentic local main dishes for under $5 and extremely cheap drinks.

If you're into camping Check out Camping Rialto - just a 10 minute bus ride in to the city centre with sites from $25.

Where to book the cheapest luxury hotels

If you want to stay in a pre-booked hotel, 'blind book'. You don't know the name of the hotel before you book. Use Last Minute Top Secret hotels and you can find a four star hotel from $80 a night in Venice!

AVOID The weekend price hike in peak season

Hostel and hotel prices skyrocket during weekends in peak season. If you can get out of Venice for the weekend if you visit in the peak season you'll save $$$ on your accommodation. For example a dorm room at a popular Hostel costs $44 a night during the week. That price goes to $253 for Saturday's and Sundays.

Local Discount Accommodation

Aside from Booking and Airbnb you can find discount b and b's on this local site: https://www.bed-and-breakfast.it/en/venice

A note on the entrance fee for day-trippers to Venice from 2023

'Venice will oblige day-trippers to make reservations and pay a fee to visit the historic lagoon city, in an attempt to better manage visitors who often far outnumber residents in the historic centre. Venice officials on Friday unveiled new rules for day-trippers, which will be in effect from 16 January 2023. Tourists who choose not to stay overnight in hotels or other lodgings will have to sign up online for the day they plan to come and pay a fee, ranging from €3 to €10 (£2.58 to £8.62) a person, depending on advance booking and whether it is peak season or the city is very crowded. Transgressors risk fines as high as €300 if they are stopped and unable to show proof they booked and paid with a QR code.' Excerpt from The Guardian.

The fee is administered by the Venice City Council but the platform they have outlined is not live at the time of writing. You can find up to date information here: https://www.veneziaunica.it/

If you're staying inside Venice you pay this tax at your accommodation.

Hack your Venice Accommodation

Your two biggest expenses when travelling to Venice are accommodation and food. This section is intended to help you cut these costs dramatically before and while you are in Venice.

Hostels are the cheapest accommodation in Venice but there are some creative workarounds to upgrade your stay on the cheap.

Use Time

There are two ways to use time. One is to book in advance. Three months will net you the best deal, especially if your visit coincides with an event. The other is to book on the day of your stay. This is a risky move, but if executed well, you can lay your head in a five-star hotel for a 2-star fee.

Before you travel to Venice, check for big events using a simple google search 'What's on in Venice', if you find no big events drawing travellers, risk showing up with no accommodation booked (If there are big events on, demand exceeds supply and you should avoid using this strategy). Start checking for discount rooms at 11 am using a private browser on booking.com.

Before I go into demand-based pricing, take a moment to think about your risk tolerance. By risk, I am not talking about personal safety. No amount of financial savings is worth risking that. What I am talking about is being inconvenienced. Do you deal well with last-minute changes? Can you roll with the punches or do you freak out if something changes? Everyone is different and knowing yourself is the best way to plan a great trip. If you are someone that likes to have everything pre-planned using demand-based pricing to get cheap accommodation will not work for you. Skip this section and go to blind-booking.

Demand-based pricing

Be they an Airbnb host or hotel manager; no one wants empty rooms. Most will do anything to make some revenue because they still have the same costs to cover whether the room is occupied or not. That's why you will find many hotels drastically slashing room rates for same-day bookings.

How to book five-star hotels for a two-star price

You will not be able to find these discounts when the demand exceeds the supply. So if you're visiting during the peak season, or during an event which has drawn many travellers again don't try this.

On the day of your stay, visit booking.com (which offers better discounts than Kayak and agoda.com). Hotel Tonight individually checks for any last-minute bookings, but they take a big chunk of the action, so the better deals come from booking.com. The best results come from booking between 2 pm and 4 pm when the risk of losing any revenue with no occupancy is most pronounced, so algorithms supporting hotels slash prices. This is when you can find rates that are not within the "lowest publicly visible" rate. To avoid losing customers to other websites, or cheapening the image of their hotel most will only offer the super cheap rates during a two hour window from 2 pm to 4 pm. Two guests will pay 10x difference in price but it's absolutely vital to the hotel that neither knows it.

Takeaway: To get the lowest price book on the day of stay between 2 pm and 4 pm and extend your search radius to include further afield hotels with good transport connections.

Priceline Hack to get a Luxury Hotel on the Cheap

Priceline.com has been around since 1997 and is an incredible site for sourcing luxury Hotels on the cheap in Venice. If you've tried everything else and that's failed, priceline will deliver.

Priceline have a database of the lowest price a hotel will accept for a particular time and date. That amount changes depending on two factors:

1. Demand: More demand high prices.
2. Likelihood of lost revenue: if the room is still available at 3pm the same-day prices will plummet.

Obviously they don't want you to know the lowest price as they make more commission the higher the price you pay.

They offer two good deals to entice you to book with them in Venice. And the good news is neither require last-minute booking (though the price will decrease the closer to the date you book).

'Firstly, 'price-breakers'. You blind book from a choice of three highly rated hotels which they name. Pricebreakers, travelers are shown three similar, highly-rated hotels, listed under a single low price.' After you book they reveal the name of the hotel.

Secondly, the 'express deals'. These are the last minute deals. You'll be able to see the name of the hotel before you book.

To find the right luxury hotel for you at a cheap price you should plug in the neighbourhoods you want to stay in, an acceptable rating (4 or 5 stars), and filter by the amenities you want.

You can also get an addition discount for your Venice hotel by booking on their dedicated app.

Hotels with frequent last-minute booking discounts:

Here are several four and five-star hotels that offer comfortable accommodations, are centrally located, and frequently have heavy last-minute booking discounts. We have included the regular pricing for comparison:

1. Hotel Belle Arti: Located in the trendy Dorsoduro neighborhood, this hotel offers comfortable rooms at an affordable price. It's within walking distance to the Peggy Guggenheim Collection and the Accademia Bridge. €80 per night.
2. Hotel Carlton on the Grand Canal: This hotel boasts a prime location on the Grand Canal, with stunning views of the waterway. The rooms are elegantly decorated. €90 per night.
3. Hotel Rialto: This historic hotel is located near the famous Rialto Bridge and offers affordable four-star ac-

commodations. The rooms are spacious and feature traditional Venetian decor. €80 per night.
4. Hotel Giorgione: This charming hotel is located in the quiet Cannaregio neighborhood, away from the crowds of tourists. The rooms are well-appointed and feature period furniture. €70 per night.
5. Hotel Santa Chiara: This hotel is located in the Santa Croce neighborhood, just a few steps from the bus and train station. It offers affordable rooms with traditional Venetian decor. €70 per night.

Pro tip: Apps like HotelTonight and Hopper also offer last-minute deals on hotels, including four-star properties in Venice.

How to trick travel Algorithms to get the lowest hotel price

Do not believe anyone who says changing your IP address to get cheaper hotels or flights does NOT work. If you don't believe us, download a Tor Network and search for flights and hotels to one destination using your current IP and then the tor network (a tor browser hides your IP address from algorithms. It is commonly used by hackers). You will receive different prices.

The price you see is a decision made by an algorithm that adjusts prices using data points such as past bookings, remaining capacity, average demand and the probability of selling the room or flight later at a higher price. If knows you've searched for the area before ip the prices high. To circumvent this, you can either use a different IP address from a cafe or airport or data from an international sim. I use a sim from Three, which provides free data in many countries around the world. When you search from a new IP address, most of the time, and particularly near booking you will get a lower price. Sometimes if your sim comes from a 'rich' country, say the UK or USA, you will see higher rates as the algorithm has learnt people from these countries pay more. The solution is to book from a local wifi connection - but a different one from the one you originally searched from.

How to get last-minute discounts on owner rented properties

In addition to Airbnb, you can also find owner rented rooms and apartments on www.vrbo.com or HomeAway or a host of others.
Nearly all owners renting accommodation will happily give renters a "last-minute" discount to avoid the space sitting

empty, not earning a dime.

Go to Airbnb or another platform and put in today's date. Once you've found something you like start the negotiating by asking for a 25% reduction. A sample message to an Airbnb host might read:

Dear HOST NAME,

I love your apartment. It looks perfect for me. Unfortunately, I'm on a very tight budget. I hope you won't be offended, but I wanted to ask if you would be amenable to offering me a 25% discount for tonight, tomorrow and the following day? I see that you aren't booked. I can assure you, I will leave your place exactly the way I found it. I will put bed linen in the washer and ensure everything is clean for the next guest. I would be delighted to bring you a bottle of wine to thank you for any discount that you could offer.

If this sounds okay, please send me a custom offer, and I will book straight away.

YOUR NAME.

In my experience, a polite, genuine message like this, that proposes reciprocity will be successful 80% of the time. Don't ask for more than 25% off, this person still has to pay the bills and will probably say no as your stay will cost them more in bills than they make. Plus starting higher, can offend the owner and do you want to stay somewhere, where you have offended the host?

In Practice
To use either of these methods, you must travel light. Less stuff means greater mobility, everything is faster and you don't have to check-in or store luggage. If you have a lot of luggage, you're going to have fewer of these opportunities to save on accommodation. Plus travelling light benefits the planet - you're buying, consuming, and transporting less stuff.

Blind-booking
If your risk tolerance does not allow for last-minute booking, you can use blind-booking. Many hotels not wanting to cheapen their brand with known low-prices, choose to operate a blind booking policy. This is where you book without knowing the name of the hotel you're going to stay in until you've made the payment. This is also sometimes used as a marketing strategy where the hotel is seeking to recover from past issues. I've stayed in plenty of blind book hotels. As long as you choose 4 or 5 star hotels, you will find them to be clean, comfortable and safe. priceline.com, Hot Rate® Hotels and Top Secret Hotels (operated by last-minute.com) offer the best deals.

Hotels.com Loyalty Program
This is currently the best hotel loyalty program with hotels in Venice. The basic premise is you collect 10 nights and get 1 free. hotels.com price match, so if booking.com has a cheaper price you can get hotel.com, to match. If you intend to travel more than ten nights in a year, its a great choice to get the 11th free.

Don't let time use you.
Rigidity will cost you money. You pay the price you're willing to pay, not the amount it requires a hotel to deliver. Therefore if you're in town for a big event, saving money on accommodation is nearly impossible so in such cases book three months ahead.

Cheapest Guesthouses in Venice

Staying in a guesthouse can provide a unique and authentic experience. They often reflect the Venice's rich cultural heritage, with traditional furnishings and décor and thus give you a more immersive experience of the local culture than a generic hotel. Here are the cheapest and best guesthouses in Venice with rooms from just $30 a night!

1. Albergo Casa Peron: This guesthouse is located in the quiet Cannaregio neighborhood, and offers basic accommodation.
2. Ca' del Gallo: This guesthouse is located in the San Marco neighborhood, just a short walk from St. Mark's Square. It offers comfortable rooms at a budget-friendly price.
3. Albergo San Samuele: This guesthouse is located in the San Marco neighborhood, close to many popular attractions.
4. B&B Ca' Dor: This guesthouse is located in the Cannaregio neighborhood, and offers cozy rooms with traditional Venetian decor.
5. Albergo Marin: This guesthouse is located in the Castello neighborhood. It's within walking distance to many popular attractions, including the Arsenale.

The best price performance location in Venice

A room putting Venice's attractions, restaurants, and nightlife within walking distance will save you time and money on transport. However restaurants and bars get much cheaper the further you go from famous tourist attractions like St Marks Square.

You will also get a better idea of the day to day life of a local if you stay on an island like Giudecca (the cheapest). For the tourist experience stay near the centre either in a last-minute hotel or Airbnb. For a taste of local life the leafy area of Cannaregio is the best you will find.

What to do if you only find overpriced options

If when you're searching for accommodation, you can only find overpriced offers, it's likely that you're visiting at a time where demand outstrips supply. In this case, have a look at www.trustedhousesitters.com. You stay for free when you care for someones pets. If you really can't find a good deal, this can be worth doing but only you know if you want to make a commitment to care for someone else's pets while on vacation. Some find it relaxing, others don't. The properties in Venice can be even more stunning than five-star hotels but if you're new to house sitting you might be against 10+ applicants, so make sure your profile is really strong before you apply for a sit. It could save you a small fortune and, who knows, you could even make some new (furry and non-furry) friends.

How to be a green tourist in Venice

Venice is sinking. Over the last 100 years the marshy land the city sits on has sunk 11 inches. The spectacular epicentre of Venice, St Mark's Square, floods more than - it flooded 4 times a year in 1900. So it's important to be a green tourist whilst in Venice to not add to our planets woes.
(If you're interested in possible solutions to stop Venice sinking read:)
There is a bizarre misconception that you have to spend money to travel in an eco-friendly way. This like, all marketing myths was concocted and hyped by companies seeking to make money off of you. In my experience, anything with eco in front of the names e.g Eco-tours will be triple the cost of the regular tour. Don't get me wrong sometimes its best to take these tours if you're visiting endangered areas, but normally such places have extensive legislation that everyone, including the eco and non-eco tour companies, are complying with. The vast majority of ways you can travel eco-friendly are free and even save you money:

- Avoid Bottled Water - get a good water bottle and refill. The water in Venice is safe to drink.

- Thrift shop but check the labels and don't buy polyester clothes - overtime plastic is released into the ocean when we wash polyester.

- Don't put your shopping in a plastic bag, bring a cotton tote with you when you venture out.

- Pack Light - this is one of the best ways to save money. If you find a 5-star hotel for tonight for $10, and you're at an Airbnb or hostel, you can easily pack and upgrade hassle-free. A light pack equals freedom and it means less to wash.

- Travel around Venice on Bikes or e-Scooters or use Public Transportation. Car Pool with services like bla bla car or Uber/Lyft share.

- Walk, this is the best way to get to know Venice. You never know what's around the corner.

It's also worth adding that there are a litany of ways tourists can be fined up to $500 in Venice:

- Littering
- Swimming in canals
- Walking shirtless

Saving money on Venice Food

Use 'Too Good To Go'

Venice offers plenty of food bargains; if you know where to look. Thankfully the app 'Too Good to Go' is turning visitors into locals by showing them exactly where to find the tastiest deals and simultaneously rescue food that would otherwise be wasted. In Venice you can pick up a $15 buy of baked goods, groceries, breakfast, brunch, lunch or dinner boxes for $2.99. You'll find lots of fish and meat dishes on offer in Venice, which would normally be expensive.

How it works? You pay for a magic bag (essentially a bag of what the restaurant or bakery has leftover) on the app and simply pick it up from the bakery or restaurant during the time they've selected. You can find extremely cheap breakfast, lunch, dinner and even groceries this way. Simply download the app and press 'my current location' to find the deals near you in Venice. .What's not to love about restafood thats a quarter of the normal price and helping to drive down food waste?

An oft-quoted parable is 'There is no such thing as cheap food. Either you pay at the cash registry or the doctor's office'. This dismisses the fact that good nutrition is a choice; we all make every-time we eat. Cheap eats are not confined to hotdogs and kebabs. The great thing about using Too Good To Go is you can eat nutritious food cheaply: fruits, vegetables, fish and nut dishes are a fraction of their supermarket cost.

Japan has the longest life expectancy in the world. A national study by the Japanese Ministry of Internal Affairs and Communications revealed that between January and May 2019, a household of two spent on average ¥65,994 a month, that's $10 per person per day on food. You truly don't need to spend a lot to eat nutritious food. That's a marketing gimmick hawkers of overpriced muesli bars want you to believe.

Never pick up a bag with a rating lower than 4.2 on the Too Good To Go app. People using it tend to be kinder because its fighting food waster. PLEASE don't waste your time on places with a rating below 4.2.

Here are some vendors in Venice that have received the best reviews on the Too Good To Go app:

- La Tecia Vegana: This vegan restaurant offers a range of plant-based dishes, including pasta, salads, and soups..
- Antico Panificio: This bakery offers a variety of fresh bread, pastries, and cakes.
- Pizzeria Ai Nomboli: This pizzeria offers traditional Neapolitan-style pizza made with high-quality ingredients.
- Aromi & Sapori: This deli offers a variety of Italian specialties, including cheeses, meats, and pasta. Users have commented on the high quality of the food received through the app, with some noting that they received a generous amount of food for the price.
- Pasta&Pasta: This pasta shop offers a variety of fresh pasta dishes, including classic Italian favorites like lasagna and carbonara.

Breakfast
If you stay somewhere with a free breakfast, eat smart. Don't eat sugary cereals or white flour rich pastries if you

don't want to be hungry an hour later. Before leaving your hotel or checking out, find some fresh fruit, water, and granola in the fitness centre or coffee in the lobby or business centre. If your hotel doesn't have free breakfast, don't take it. You can always eat cheaper outside.

Al 133 (Address: Salizada San Pantalon, 133) has the best cheap breakfast we found. Here you can pick up buttery croissants for less than $1.

Visit supermarkets at discount times.
You can get a 50 per cent discount around 5 pm at the Conrad supermarkets on fresh produce. The cheaper the supermarket, the less discounts you will find, so check Conrad and at 5 pm. Some items are also marked down due to sell-by date after the lunchtime rush so its also worth to check in around 3 pm.

Street vendors

You can also find street vendors selling food throughout the city, including breakfast options like hot sandwiches and crepes. Look for these vendors in popular squares and markets.

Festivals & Events

Carnevale in February - Masquerade madness stretches over two weeks in February before Lent. Carnevale is magical. There are people in costumes and hundreds of boat parades.

Venice International Film Festival held from August through to the first week of September.

Is the tap water drinkable?
Yes. There are over 100 drinking fountains in Venice with good, safe, free water to refill your bottle.

How much can you save haggling here?
Gondola drivers have a set price, so will only negotiate up from 80 euros. Especially if you look like a rich tourist. Market vendors are open to negotiation, depending on footfall.

SNAPSHOT: How to enjoy a $5,000 trip to Venice for $300

(full breakdown at the end of the guide)

Stay	Travelling in peak season: 1. Last-minute hotels via priceline.com express deals 2. Stay in a private room in a Airbnb if you want privacy and cooking facilities. 3. Stay in hostels if you want to meet over travellers. Generator Venice is amazing value and has a cheap kitchen. 4. Housesit. Travelling in low season 1. Last minute five-star hotels.
Eat	You don't need to spend a fortune in Venice to eat memorable food. Average meal cost: $6 - $12. Use Too Good To Go for a couple of restaurant dinners to save $200+
Move	Water bus - Vaporetto - $40 for unlimited travel for 3 days.
See	Get the St Mark's Square Museum Card $18. With this you can get away with spending less than $20 in entrance fees.
Experience	Getting lost in Venice, Gondolas, rooftop bars and beaches
Total	300 US$

Unique bargains I love in Venice

Venice has the reputation of being among the most luxurious and expensive destinations in the world. Fortunately, some of the best things in life are free or cheap. You can pick up a litre of good red wine for $2! the so called Vino Sfuso meaning loose wine. Venice is full of bargains when you know where to look and where to AVOID! Eat in either or - the food is great and cheap and there's no chance of being conned in these less touristy islands.

The first thing you should do when you arrive in Venice to see what free events are on during your stay. Many use free food and drink to entice people: https://www.eventbrite.com/d/italy--venezia/free--events/

Venice is always crowded with tourists. When you're in need of escaping the crowds to somewhere green hop off the water bus at Torcello, Mazzorbo, Sant'Erasmo or Le Vignole. There are parks and stretches of green there. Plus the first village built in the Lagoon was not Venice but Torcello, by people fleeing the Barbarians, so its great for history fanatics.

If you have one, Take your student card
Venice offers hundreds of student discounts. If you're studying buy an ISIC card - International Student Identity Card. It's a great investment because its valid in 133 countries and covers 150,000 discounts including many hundreds in Venice.

Senior discounts
Nearly every major museum, attraction and The Vaporetto offers reduced fares for seniors age 65.

How to use this book

Google and TripAdvisor are your on-the-go guides while traveling, a travel guide adds the most value during the planning phase, and if you're without Wi-Fi. Always download the google map for your destination - having an offline map will make using this guide much more comfortable. For ease of use, we've set the book out the way you travel, booking your flights, arriving, how to get around, then on to the money-saving tips. The tips we ordered according to when you need to know the tip to save money, so free tours and combination tickets feature first. We prioritized the rest of the tips by how much money you can save and then by how likely it was that you could find the tip with a google search. Meaning those we think you could find alone are nearer the bottom. I hope you find this layout useful. If you have any ideas about making Super Cheap Insider Guides easier to use, please email me philgattang@gmail.com

A quick note on How We Source Super Cheap Tips
We focus entirely on finding the best bargains. We give each of our collaborators $2,000 to hunt down never-before-seen deals. The type you either only know if you're local or by on the ground research. We spend zero on marketing and a little on designing an excellent cover. We do this yearly, which means we just keep finding more amazing ways for you to have the same experience for less.

Now let's get started with juicing the most pleasure from your trip to Venice with the least possible money!

OUR SUPER CHEAP TIPS...

Here are our specific tips to enjoy a $5,000 trip to Venice for $300

How to Find Super Cheap Flights to Venice

Luck is just an illusion. Anyone can find incredible flight deals. If you can be flexible you can save huge amounts of money. In fact, the biggest tip I can give you for finding incredible flight deals is simple: find a flexible job. Don't despair if you can't do that theres still a lot you can do. The following pages detail the exact method I use to consistently find cheap flights to Venice.

Book your flight to Venice on a Tuesday or Wednesday

Tuesdays and Wednesdays are the cheapest days of the week to fly. You can take a flight to Venice on a Tuesday or Wednesday for less than half the price you'd pay on a Thursday Friday, Saturday, Sunday or Monday.

Start with Google Flights (but NEVER book through it!)

I conduct upwards of 50 flight searches a day for readers. I use google flights first when looking for flights. I put specific departure but broad destination (e.g Europe) and usually find amazing deals.

The great thing about Google Flights is you can search by class. You can pick a specific destination and it will tell you which time is cheapest in which class. Or you can put in dates and you can see which area is cheapest to travel to.

But be aware Google flights does not show the cheapest prices among the flight search engines but it does offer several advantages

1. You can see the cheapest dates for the next 8 weeks. Other search engines will blackout over 70% of the prices.
2. You can put in multiple airports to fly from. Just use a common to separate in the from input.
3. If you're flexible on where you're going Google flights can show you the cheapest destinations.
4. You can set-up price tracking, where Google will email you when prices rise or decline.

Once you have established the cheapest dates to fly go over to skyscanner.net and put those dates in. You will find sky scanner offers the cheapest flights.

Get Alerts when Prices to Venice are Lowest

Google also has a nice feature which allows you to set up an alert to email you when prices to your destination are at their lowest. So if you don't have fixed dates this feature can save you a fortune.

Baggage add-ons

It may be cheaper and more convenient to send your luggage separately with a service like sendmybag.com Often the luggage sending fee is cheaper than what the airlines charge to check baggage. Visit Lugless.com or luggagefree.com in addition to sendmybag.com for a quotation.

Loading times

Anyone who has attempted to find a cheap flight will know the pain of excruciating long loading times. If you encounter this issue use google flights to find the cheapest dates and then go to skyscanner.net for the lowest price.

Always try to book direct with the airline

Once you have found the cheapest flight go direct to the airlines booking page. This is advantageous in the current covid cancellation climate, because if you need to change your flights or arrange a refund, its much easier to do so, than via a third party booking agent.

That said, sometimes the third party bookers offer cheaper deals than the airline, so you need to make the decision based on how likely you think it is that disruption will impede you making those flights.

More flight tricks and tips

www.secretflying.com/usa-deals offers a range of deals from the USA and other countries. For example you can pick-up a round trip flight non-stop from from the east coast to johannesburg for $350 return on this site

Scott's cheap flights, you can select your home airport and get emails on deals but you pay for an annual subscription. A free workaround is to download Hopper and set search alerts for trips/price drops.

Premium service of Scott's cheap flights.
They sometime have discounted business and first class but in my experience they are few and far between.

JGOOT.com has 5 times as many choices as Scott's cheap flights.

kiwi.com allows you to be able to do radius searches so you can find cheaper flights to general areas.

Finding Error Fares
Travel Pirates (www.travelpirates.com) is a gold-mine for finding error deals. Subscribe to their newsletter. I recently found a reader an airfare from Montreal-Brazil for a $200 round trip (mistake fare!). Of course these error fares are always certain dates, but if you can be flexible you can save a lot of money.

Things you can do that might reduce the fare to Venice:--
- Use a VPN (if the booker knows you booked one-way, the return fare will go up)
- Buy your ticket in a different currency

How to Find CHEAP FIRST-CLASS Flights to Venice

Upgrade at the airport
Airlines are extremely reluctant to advertise price drops in first or business class tickets so the best way to secure them is actually at the airport when airlines have no choice but to decrease prices dramatically because otherwise they lose money. Ask about upgrading to business or first-class when you check-in. If you check-in online look around the airport for your airlines branded bidding system. For example KLM at Amsterdam have terminals where you can bid on upgrades.

Use Air-miles

When it comes to accruing air-miles for American citizens **Chase Sapphire Reserve card** ranks top. If you put everything on there and pay it off immediately you will end up getting free flights all the time, aside from taxes.

Get 2-3 chase cards with sign up bonuses, you'll have 200k points in no time and can book with points on multiple airlines when transferring your points to them.

Please note, this is only applicable to those living in the USA. In the Bonus Section we have detailed the best air-mile credit cards for those living in the UK, Canada, Germany, Austria, Spain and Australia.

How many miles does it take to fly first class?
First class from Bangkok to Chicago (one way) costs 180,000 miles.

Cheapest route to Venice from America

At the time of writing Norwegian are flying to Rome for around $300 return. The cheapest route to Venice is via Rome, from there you can take a 5 hour bus for $9 to Venice. If you want to go direct you can pick up flights with TAP Air for $450 return from NYC.

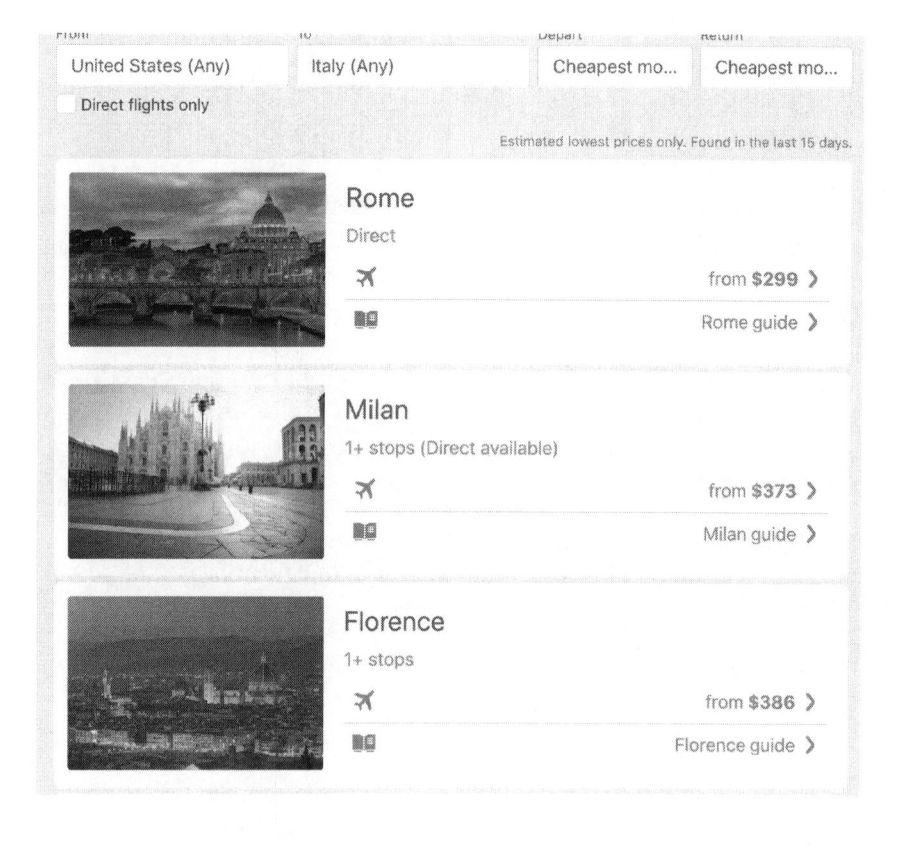

Arriving

Get a vaporetto (water bus) pass to get around. It costs $40 for unlimited travel for 3 days. Otherwise the cost is $15 for one single trip. You take a bus into Venice from the airport. Cost one way is 6 euros per person. From Piazza Roma (bus terminal) you need to catch the vaporetto (water boat) to your island.

INSIDER HISTORICAL INSIGHT
Did you know? Venezuela is named after Venice. Venezuela means 'little Venice' in Spanish. In 1499 Amerigo Vespucci, a Venetian explorer landed on the Venezuelan coast. The stilt houses of Lake Maracaibo reminded the Italian navigator of Venice…

Need a place to store luggage?
Use stasher.com to find a convenient place to store your luggage cheaply. It provides much cheaper options than airport and train station lockers in Venice.

Getting around

The city is divided into six sestieri (districts): Cannaregio, Castello, San Marco, Dorsoduro, San Polo and Santa Croce use the Vaporetto to get between them.
The water buses - Vaporetto - are super easy to navigate between the islands and are quite fun to just ride around.

Prices for the regular Vaporetto: Single fare 7 Euros
Travelcard 12 hours 18 €
Travelcard 24 hours 20 €
Travelcard 36 hours 25 €
Travelcard 48 hours 30 €
Travelcard 72 hours 40 €
Travelcard 7 Days 50 €
You can buy those tickets and passes either from their ticket office or from the ticket vending machines at most larger Vaporetto stations. Before boarding for the first time, validate your ticket at the little yellow machine at the stop. You

can be fined one-thespot for travelling with an unvalidated ticket. You only need to validate it once.
Wynn, Michael. ONE-TWO-GO Venice: The Ultimate Guide to Venice 2016 with Helpful Maps, Breathtaking Photos and Insider Advice (One-Two-Go.com Book 17) . One-Two-Go.com. Kindle Edition.

INSIDER MONEY SAVING TIP
If you are craving the perfect postcard photo of Venice go outside Hotel Bauer. It has everything, a great view of the canal, a bridge… and many gondolas passing serenely.

Drive - there's an app called 'KINTO' which allows you to rent a car from $0.19 per minute + more for the Kilometre's but its cheaper than a car rental and you can do hourly, daily or even weekly packages. You just scan the QR code on the code, hop in and drive.

Start with a ride on Number 1

The Number 1 Line cruises from one end of the Grand Canal to the other on a 45 minute scenic sail. Most of the fabulous landmarks like the Piazza san Marco with its nearby Basilicas, the Doge's Palace, the Rialto Bridge, the Basilica Santa Maria and many more of the top sights are dotted along Number 1's route.

INSIDER HISTORICAL INSIGHT
'Ciao' originated in Venice. The Venetian greeting, "s-ciavo vostro", translates to "your slave". The greeting was shortened over the years to "ciao".

Walk Venice

Never underestimate the entertainment of simply walking around Venice. This should be your main mode of transport. Venice is a city that richly rewards those who explore her charms on vote. When Google maps has no clue of where you are. Don't despair, follow the crowds if you ever feel truly lost. The main tourist area is between Santa Lucia train station (signposted as the ferrovia) and Piazza San Marco (St Mark's Sq). The path between the two – Venice's main drag – is a 50-minute walk. Even with a smartphone and satellite mapping you're bound to get lost, but you're have fun doing so.

INSIDER HISTORICAL INSIGHT
The first settlers of Venice were refugees escaping Germanic and Barbarian invasions in Roman cities. They first settled in Torcello and Lido, to later move to what it is actually known as Rialto.

INSIDER MONEY SAVING TIP
Aqua Alta Bookshop (Libreria Acqua Alta) on Castello is one of the most beautiful bookstores in the world. The terrace has a set of beautiful book steps, which make for great portrait photos.

Orientate yourself with this free tour

Forget exploring Venice by wandering around aimlessly. Start with a free organised tour. Nothing compares to local advice, especially when travelling on a budget. Ask for their recommendations for the best cheap eats, the best bargains, the best markets, the best place for a particular street eat. Perhaps some of it will be repeated from this guide, but it can't hurt to ask, especially if you have specific needs or questions. At the end you should leave an appropriate tip (usually around $5), but nobody bats an eye lid if you are unable or unwilling to do so, tell them you will leave a good review and always give them a little gift from home - I always carry small Vienna fridge magnets and I always tip the $5, but it is totally up to you.

This is the free tour I did. I thought it was a great introduction to the city and covered all the main attractions. You can book here: https://venicefreewalkingtour.com/

A note on paying for tours
The only time paying for a tour is worth it, is when you couldn't reach the place without the tour (e.g you need a boat), or when the tour is about the same price as the attraction entry. Otherwise you can do a range of self-guided tours using for FREE.

INSIDER MONEY SAVING TIP
If you have more time Try Geocaching. This is where you hunt for hide-and-seek containers. You need a mobile device to follow the GPS clues in Venice. A typical cache is a small, waterproof container with a logbook where you can leave a message or see various trinkets left by other cache hunters. Build your own treasure hunt by discovering geocaches in Venice.

Visit Free Museums

The average traveller spends $180 on museums in Venice but there's no need to spend a dime if you time your trip to visit on the free days. To ensure everybody has access to culture Venice's state-run museums are free on the first Sunday of each month: Here are the best of the crop:

• Gallerie del- l'Accademia - pre-19th-century art.
• Galleries at Ca' D'oro - Renaissance antiquities, plus art by Tit- ian & Van Dyck displayed in an ornate, 15th-century palace

- National Archaeological Museum of Venice - National archaeo-logical Museum housing ancient Egyptian, Greek, Roman & Babylonian antiquities.
- Oriental Art Museum
- Grimani Palace Museum - Elegant palazzo of Venice's former ruler.

Cruise the Grand Canal

Its the major water-traffic corridor and a stunning sight to behold. The Vaporetto go up and down it constantly and with your pass you can use it endlessly giving a great vantage point for snaps.

Buy the St Mark's Square Museum Card

You get free entry into 4 museums for $18. Doge's Palace, Museo Correr, Archaeology Musuem and the Monumental rooms of the marciana National Library. Saving you $30 and time queuing. There's a lot of online scams for this ticket, so only buy it at the ticket office. Go at 9am to avoid queuing.

INSIDER MONEY SAVING TIP
You can buy an online voucher for timed entrance to avoid the long lines for only 1.5 Euros:

Tips for saving money in St Marks Square

Many of the things you will want to see are around St Marks Square - Piazza San Marco. Here are some need-to-knows before you go:

Do NOT EAT in St. Marks Square prices can go into the hundreds for a glass of wine.

Do NOT EAT at any place advertising in multiple languages - its a tourist trap. Look for a 'bacaro' (tavern). These neighbourhood pubs offer simple fare, usually with handwritten menus or none at all but are cheap and delicious.

DON'T sit down for an espresso or a cappuccino. Coffee bars will charge you an extra fee to sit down and serve you. It's called a coperto and it's at every restaurant in Italy.

St. Mark's Basilica

Construction began here in 1063. Book the hidden treasures tour. You get access to places in the Basilica you can't get access to with private tours. It is 21.50 but worth every penny.

St. Mark's Basilica looks even more beautiful at night, so come back in the evening too.

Doge's Palace

Initially built as a castle, this palace became home to the Duke, the highest political rank in Venice. It was then the cities political hub for centuries. Today it's the most popular attraction in Venice, and entry will cost you 9.50 euros or is free with the St Mark's Square Museum Card.

Enjoy a Gondola ride for 2 euros

Gondola rides are not budget friendly, at a set rate of €80 for 40 minutes it is best to find a group if you want to take one. If you don't want to share a ride, you can stand on the traghetto (public gondola) as you cross the Grand Canal for €2. Just look for a yellow sign with the black gondola symbol and ask for the Traghetto.

Try Venice Tapas

Now we've mentioned what not to eat, lets talk about what you should eat: Cicheti! Venice Tapas served at lunch and from around 6pm to 8pm with Veneto wines by the glass. They range from basic bar snacks (spicy meatballs, fresh tomato and basil bruschetta) to highly inventive small plates:
Try All'Arco at 56 66; Calle dell'Ochialer 436, San Polo; serves them from €2.

Get a panini from Bar Alla Toletta for $3.
This little find is a rare cheap eat gem.
Address: Dorsoduro, 1191,

Dal Moros Fresh Pasta to Go.
You choose your pasta and sauce - it's €6 on average) and probably the best pasta I ever had in Italy.

INSIDER MONEY SAVING TIP
Campo Santa Margherita is a Piazza surrounded by restaurants, bars, and cheap food stalls, it is where the workers of Venice eat. You find some of the best cheap eats here.

Eat the best Gelato

Go to Suso. This gelato is made with local ingredients and following the seasons. You can indulge in a mascarpone gelato and 100's more flavours from 1.60 euros.
: Calle della Bissa, 5453.

Grab a large water bottle and fill it up with wine for 2 euros

There are a few wine shops in where you can buy wine from a barrel poured into your own container. Look for the sign 'Vino sfuso' loose wine. You can get a litre for 2.10 euros. I brought mine from Cantinone Gìa Schiavi In . Cantinone già Schiavi sells their house wine sfuso too. It changes depending on the season. **Google Vino Sfuso Venice to see who is selling it during your visit.**

Church Hop

Not only exceptional architecturally and historically, Venice churches contain exquisite art, artefacts and other priceless treasures. Best of all, entry to the lessor known ones is, in most cases, free. Basilica di Santa Maria della Salute built to offer thanks for Venice's salvation from plague, is free to explore.

The Church of San Giorgio Maggiore is a Palladian church overlooking the lagoon that's free to enter and breathtakingly beautiful.
Address: Isola di S.Giorgio Maggiore, 30133.

Santa Maria dei Miracoli is a 15th century church hidden in Castello Area, unlike all the other churches in Venice, it has remained practically untouched,. The architecture is incredible, with both interior and facades sculpted multi-coloured marble.

INSIDER MONEY SAVING TIP

Convento di San Francesco del Deserto is a monastery where Franciscan friars offer delightful free tours of their secluded home. Book your tour here: http://www.san-francescodeldeserto.it/

Visit Cannnaregio

Home to the Jewish ghetto, great cheap bars and markets minus the crowds on San Marco. It makes for a lovely, less crowded afternoon walk.

INSIDER HISTORICAL INSIGHT
Cannnaregio was originally the seat of a metal foundry ('geti' in Italian), before it became a residential area for Christians in the 15th century. In 1516, the Venetian authorities threw them out and forced all Jews to live there in confinement.

Enjoy a beach day (weather permitting)

Lido is 20 minutes from Venice via the Vaparetto. Take a towel, sun lotion, and your swimming gear for a dip. In July and August it is absolutely heaving, so go early to get your spot. Go on Tuesdays for a great Tuesday produce market and free Tuesday summer concerts.

Go to where it all began

Most tourists never visit Torcello, which is a shame given that is just five-minute vaporetto ride from Burano and home to the first ancient settlements of the lagoon. If you visit you're be rewarded with the Basilica di Santa Maria Assunta (there are amazing big Byzantine mosaic inside the Basilica), Santa Fosca church and the "Devil's bridge" (Ponte del Diavolo) - one of only two still standing here.

Try **Coffee straight from the roastery**

Don't let the 1 euro stand-up espresso fool you, Italians are incredibly discerning when it comes to coffee. Torrefazione Cannaregiois is a tiny shop roasting coffee everyday. Founded in 1939, it is today the last coffee shop in Venice with an in-store roasting license. If you pick up a membership card you can get 10 coffees for €8.40 - insane value for the quality of the coffee.

Visit a 15th century architectural phenomenon

Scala Contarini del Bovolo has re-opened after generations of restoration and disagreements. It is hidden from sight, located at a dead-end 'calle' (street). It costs 7 euros to enter and offers great hidden views, a beautiful gothic staircase and is definitely worth going inside if you love arches.

Discover ancient art production for free

The Orsoni furnace was founded in 1888. Today they are singlehandedly trying to revive Byzantine mosaic art and the Renaissance Murano pure enamels. Book in advance for a Wednesday morning to visit the furnace and you will get a free guide who will tell you about how mosaic tiles are made and their importance to Venetians. Book here: They also did a great Ted Talk:

Go to a Venetian antique markets

Mercantino San Maurizio started out in 1970 offering Murano chandeliers, old postcards, vintage clothes, pocket watches, leather goods and jewellery. You can find pieces from the 1600s. The market attracts many collectors and keen bargain hunters. The dates of the market are updated here: https://www.mercatinocamposanmaurizio.it/

Visit this colourful island

Known for its unique glass art, Murano features studios, demonstrations and souvenirs for sale. It makes for a stunning backdrop for photos. Plus there are commercial art galleries and glass showrooms that you can peruse for free.

Visit the Bridge of Sighs

This infamous arched bridge dating from 1600 was named Bridge of Sighs because of the sighs of prisoners crossing it en route from the Palazzo Ducale to prison.

Visit Rialto

No visit to Venice would be complete without visiting this ornate 16th-century stone footbridge crossing the Grand Canal. Go early to explore the nearby fish market - Mercato di Rialto and escape the crowds.

Visit Burano

Colorful houses dot this lively fishing island with seafood restaurants, a lace museum and bell tower. The number 12 vaporetto goes there. Exploring Burano makes for a wonderful afternoon.

Escape the crowds

If you are easily overwhelmed by crowds plan to visit Venice during mid-week, visit the obvious attractions as early as possible, peak people flow is 10 am to 5 pm so get up early to enjoy the attractions serenely. Luckily Venice also has many hidden gems that aren't commercialized or too crowded most of the time. Avoid Rialto, San Marco and Ponte dei Suspiri and instead walk the narrow alleys in Cannaregio (Ponte Chiodo is my favourite bridge) and Santa Croce. Both have plenty of Venice photo opportunities, minus the stress of other toursts. Plus here you never know whats tucked around a corner or hidden in a cobbled alleyway.

1. Remembrance Park (Parco delle Rimembranz) is a large green space shaded by pine trees. This is a beautiful spot to relax and watch the sun go down
2. The Isola Della Certosa island is an excellent option, and offers a beautiful garden with panoramic views of Venice. You can also engage in water sports at the island, which is relatively untouched by tourists.
3. Verona and Bologna are close by train for more Italian Adventures or you could do Lake Como in a weekend (Varenna is the best village).
4. For lounging on the beach, you can't beat Pula and Rovinj, in Croatia. Which are just a short ferry ride away.

Go Book Shopping

Libreria Acqua Alta, which is a sight in its own right (as mentioned above) offers a huge range of paperback books for low prices.

Address: C. Longa Santa Maria Formosa, 5176b, 30122

Not super cheap but worth the fee

Gallerie dell'Accademia
A treasure trove of Venetian painting. Museum of 13th- to 18th-century Venetian artwork, with paintings by Titian, Canaletto & Tiepolo. Outside the free days it costs €6.50 to enter.

Peggy Guggenheim Collection
Modern art museum in 18th-century waterside palace with a 20th-century art collection & an interior sculpture garden. It costs €12 to enter.

Venice Food and drink hacks

Cicchetti
'The cicchetti take their name from the Latin ciccus which means "small quantities. They are, also called cicheti or cichéti in the Venetian dialect, got their start as little snacks or bites to accompany local red or white wine sold by wine merchants that came to the city.'

For incredible *cicchetti* - go to Taverna Del Campiello Remer from 5-7 PM.

If you're looking for a great aperitivo (free snacks with your happy hour drinks) go to Taverna Del Campiello Remer from 5-7. You pay €3, buy one drink, and get to eat as much from their little buffet as you want! It's hard to locate, so use google maps. The best way to experience Venice is by walking from one small bar to the next, having a glass of wine and a couple *cicchetti* at each. You may end up spending the price of a meal but you'll have seen 6-8 places instead of just one.

Here are the best places for *cicchetti in Venice:*

- Osteria Al Squero
- Bar Dorsoduro,
- Cantina Do Spade
- Bar All'Arco
- Cantina Do Mori

- Cantine del Vino
- acareto da Lele

Cheapest nice wine bar

El Refolo is a lovely cheap wine bar on Castello.
Sestiere Castello, 1580

La Bottiglia is another cheap wine bar with great ambience.
Address: Campo S. Stin, 2537

Best bang for your buck all-you-caneat

Mirai is a Japanese with Great food with lots of different options from seafood, meat, sushi and all you can eat for 15.9 EUR. Plus it is on the grand canal with romantic terrace dining. All you can eats are a great way to stock on on nutritious food while travelling. Dishes like fish are normally expensive, but here you can chow down on your omega 3's for much less. I know friends who take Tupperware with them to take some snacks away, personally I don't as its not ethical and karma is real. Don't drink much water or eat bread and you'll get more than your money's worth.

Address: Cannaregio, 146

Cheap Eats

It's actually quite hard to have a bad meal in Venice, but it's easy to have an overpriced one. Fill your stomach without emptying your wallet by trying these local restaurants with mains under $10 (Most of them are on Dorsoduro or
Castello).

Note: Download the offline map for Venice on Google maps, (instructions 1. go to app 2. select offline apps in the left sidebar 3. go to the area you want to download 4. click download). Then simply type the restaurant names in to navigate, add the restaurants to your favourites by clicking the star icon so you can see where the cheap eats are when you're out and about to avoid wasting your money at hyped tourist joints)

Pizza al Volo
Address: Dorsoduro, 2944
Great cheap pizza. A slice for a euro.
Rosticceria Gislon
Address: Calle de la Bissa, 5424/a
Very cheap sandwiches - expect to pay 3euros.
Antico Forno Venezia
Address: Ruga Rialto, 973
Cheap pizza takeaway place or eat inside.
Osteria Alla Ciurma
Address: Calle Galiazza, 406/A
The cichettis were really cheap!
Arte Della Pizza
Address: Calle de l'Aseo, 1861A
Small site, good pizza, Godó service and cheap.
Ostaria Dai Zemei
Traditional Venetian eatery with a counter crammed with cicchetti, plus regional wines by the glass.

Address: San Polo, 1045/b
Cheap quick bites.
Impronta Cafe Restaurant
Open all day, with sandwiches & a full menu of classic dishes, plus cocktails.
Address: Dorsoduro, 3815
They also have Great cocktails.
Osteria Al Squero
Address: Dorsoduro, 943-944
Amazing place for some cheap crostini.
Pizza 2000
Address: Campo Sant'Agostin, 2287
Best pizza I tried in Venice. Very cheap and delicious.
Osteria Antico Giardinetto
Cozy, family-run restaurant with a rustic interior & a fishcentric menu of Med/Venetian dishes.
Address: Calle dei Morti, 2253
Trattoria dalla Marisa
Address: Calle del Magazzen, 652
The food is tasty, no matter what I ate, big portions, and cheap.
Osteria Ai Osti
Address: Corte dei Pali già Testori, Calle S. Felice, 3849
Very cheap traditional lunch.
Fried Land
Address: Calle Fiori, 2287
A lot of fried stuff, but actually the food was great and cheap.
Dal Moro's Fresh Pasta To Go
Boxes of fresh pasta mixed with a pick of made-to-order sauces served in a buzzing take-out spot. The best and cheapest pasta in Venice.
Address: Calle Casseleria, 5324
Bacareto da Lele
Offers amazingly cheap paninis (sandwiches). Its a tiny place with no tables or chairs inside, but you can always sit on the nearby steps or take it standing on one of the barrels.
We Love Italy fresh pasta to go - Rialto - Venice

Address: Calle de l'Orso, 5529
Lively spot for fresh pasta to go. Great when you need a great, cheap, quick meal in Venice.
Antico Forno
Address: Rugheta del Ravano, 973
Craft beer plus pizza slices to go
Crepes House by PePe
Address: Fondamenta S. Giobbe, 549
Sweet & savory crepes to take away
Baci & Pasta
Address: Campo Santa Marina, 5902/a
Crazy pizza
Address: Salizada S. Lio, 5706
Cheapest pizza in Venice and delicious.
Pako's Pizza & Pasta
Address: Spadaria, 687
Tiny pizzeria offering takeout
Puppa Bar Venezia
Address: C. dello Spezier, 4800
Hole in the wall hidden gem incredible seafood, risotto & pasta at low-prices.

Save money on restaurants cafes with these tips

Any bar or cafe has to have their prices posted by law. And they'll have two: bar and table. If you want to save money on eating out, take away the food or drinks. This goes for coffee too. An espresso at the bar costs 1 euro. It will cost you 3 euros to drink it sitting down. All Italian restaurants charge a cover charge for the bread, oil, napkins etc, normally 3 euros.

Buy soda at the supermarket not the restaurant. A small can will cost at least 5 Euros.

Don't ask your waiter to recommend a wine, he will recommend the most expensive.

Fish: often fish is listed on the menu by weight so what looks like a $7 fish is probably more like 35 euros for the whole fish.

Need to Know before you go

Currency: Euro
Language: Italian .
Data: The best sim for Italy is with the network 'Three' because they allow you to use your data for free in 71 destinations including most of Europe.

Money: Widely available ATMs.
Visas: http://www.doyouneedvisa.com/
Time: GMT + 1
Important Numbers
113 Ambulance
112 Police

Getting Out of Venice cheaply

Flixbus

Booking ahead can save you up to 98% of the cost of the flixbus ticket. Onward destinations include most Italian cities. Prices start at just $4.

Plane

At the time of writing Wizz Air and RyanAir are offering the cheapest flights onwards. Take advantage of discounts and specials. Sign up for e-newsletters from local carriers including Wizz Air to learn about special fares. Be careful with cheap airlines, most will allow hand-luggage only, and some charge for anything that is not a backpack. Check their websites before booking if you need to take luggage.

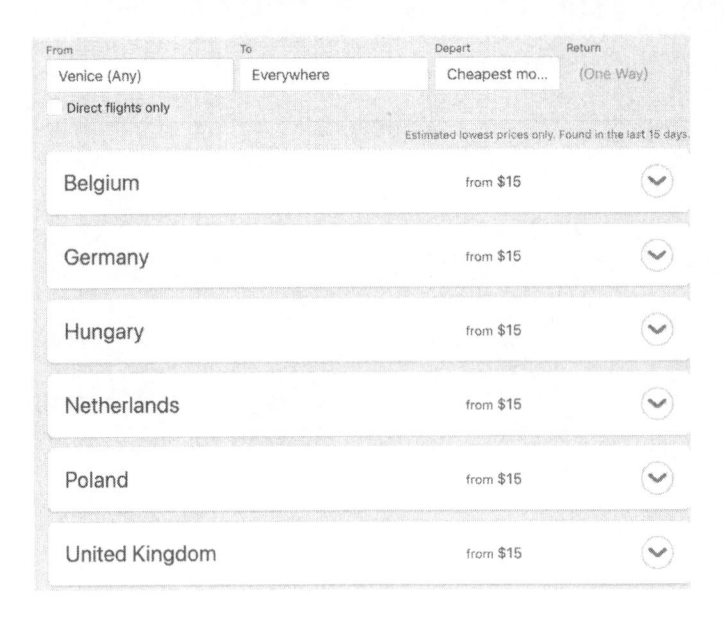

From	To	Depart	Return
Venice (Any)	Everywhere	Cheapest mo...	(One Way)

☐ Direct flights only

Estimated lowest prices only. Found in the last 15 days.

Belgium	from $15
Germany	from $15
Hungary	from $15
Netherlands	from $15
Poland	from $15
United Kingdom	from $15

Car share

BlaBlaCar is also used widely in Venice - you can share a car to Vienna for as little as $15 - blablacar.com

Airport Lounges

You don't need to be flying business or first class to enjoy an airport lounge. Here are three methods you can use to access lounges at Venice airport:

- Get or use a credit card that gives free lounge access. NerdWallet has a good write-up about cards that offer free lounge access. www.nerdwallet.com/best/credit-cards/airport-lounge-access

- Buy onetime access. They start at $23 and often include free showers and free drinks and food.

- Find free access with the LoungeBuddy app. You pay an annual fee of $25 to use the app.

Avoid these tourist traps or scams

Venice despite its tourists crowds is not scam central. Locals are too busy trying to navigate the hordes of tourists to scam them. Eat and drink in or areas for local prices and be aware of pickpockets like you would be generally. Like anywhere there are pickpockets lurking around attractions. Don't keep things in your back pockets in this or any other busy area or crowded pubs - they are opportunistic thieves rather than forceful ones.

When searching to buy tickets online always add 'Official website' to your search, many sneaky operators have constructed ticket purchasing sites which inflate the prices. ONLY BUY FROM THE OFFICIAL SITES.

Fully Costed Breakdown

	How	Cost with suggested tip
How I got from the airport to the city	Varapetto	$40 for a 3 day unlimited Vaparetto ticket
Stay x 3	Last-minute five-star hotel via priceline express deals	$60
Tastiest street foods to try	Average meal cost: $8 - see cheap eats section. Get a litre of wine for 2 euros	$8 average
Get around	Vaparetto and walking	free
See	The free sights	$0
Best discounts	St Marks Pass	$18
Get out	Wizz Air are flying to 25 EU cities for $15. Take the Flixbus to Italian cities from $5	$5
Total		$300

RECAP: How to enjoy a $5,000 trip to Venice for $300

Find a cheap flight
Using the strategy we outlined you can snag a ticket to Venice from the states from $180 return. From the EU budget carrier Ryanair is flying to Venice from $5! Potential saving $1,000.

Blind book hotels or use or accommodation finder service.
Some of the cheapest hotel deals are available when you 'blind book'. You don't know the name of the hotel before you book. Use Last Minute Top Secret hotels and or priceline express deals and you can find a four or five star hotel from $80 a night in Venice! Potential saving $3,500

Use too good to go
Save an absolute fortune on foods by picking up magic bags from over 5,000 restaurants, bakeries, ice cream parlous and supermarkets located all over Venice. And remember never buy a bag without rating and never with ratings under 4.2 stars. It's also worth noting a lot of hotels offer great breakfast buffer magic bags but some are a total waste of time in Venice. Check the reviews before purchasing. Potential saving: $500

Take advantage of Cicchetti time
Between 5 - 7pm bars in Venice give out free snacks when you buy a drink.

Buy the St Marks Museum card and do free tours
Get cultured on the cheap by doing the great free tours and buying the St Marks Museum car. The average traveller spends $80 on museums in Venice. If you do plan to see many attractions invest in the St Marks Museum card. Potential saving $60.

Drink outdoors with friends

Venice is such a beautiful city, the best way to experience the city is to buy a couple of beers from a supermarket and enjoy them somewhere green, or just by the canals. A beer costs around $5 in a bar. Potential savings on drinks $100 - hey you're on vacation, but don't let it get out of hand. By-laws mean you can be fined for rowdy behaviour.

Enjoy your first day for $20

St Marks Square at sunrise

After a croissant and espresso at Marchini Time for $2, hop on the water bus to go to Rialto. Saviour the views from the southern side of the bridge. Have a look around the centuries old fish market and then make you way to St Mark's Bascillca to start your free walking tour.
Grab a Pannini for lunch, and then complete the 4 museums you can see for free with the museum card. Ravel in getting lost in Venice and watch flush tourists part with hundreds for gondola rides. Have a $7 dinner at Dal Moros Fresh Pasta to Go. Finish the night off with cheap drinks in Campo Santa Margherita.

PRACTICAL THINGS TO REMEMBER TO SAVE MONEY

- If you really want to see Venice stay in Venice; not in Mestre. The access is worth the extra money. Pus from 2023 you'd have to pay a day access fee to the city.
- Don't feel that you need to stay near San Marco though - Venice is meant to be walked and you'll much prefer staying out of the main touristic area and walking to see the sights there. You'll also have better access to affordable food/drink.

- Buy an online voucher for timed entrance to St Mark's Basilica to avoid the long lines for only 1.5 Euros.
-
- Book the free tours you want to take BEFORE you travel. Spots fill up fast.

- Download google maps for for use offline. You will still get lost, but you'll be able to find your way back to a Vaporetto.

- Download the Italian language pack on google translate - you will be grateful you have it! The camera function is great for translating Italian menus.

- Bring a good mosquito spray or combine a few drops of lemongrass oil with a moisturiser. This is the technique the Inca's used to keep mosquitos at bay. The smell turns the mosquitos away from your skin. Mosquitos can be a big nuisance here in summer.

- Pick up food from the too good to go app - Plan to get your breakfast or dinner from restaurants on the app. $2.99 for a restaurant meal will save you at least $500 on food in Venice.

- Don't eat at any restaurants with touts outside.
- Go away from the main thoroughfares in Venice for cheaper restaurant prices
- Bring good shoes to Walk, walk, walk. If you wander most of the day, you can expect to easily walk 8+ miles in a day but you'll discover corners of the city most tourists don't find even on 7 day trips. See the Rialto and San Marco areas but spend 90% of your time elsewhere.
- Know the names of foods to try and the star the restaurants to try them at on Google Maps.
- Plan to start sightseeing early for a more serene ex•perience especially when visiting museums on their free days.
- Avoid over-scheduling. You don't want to pack so much into your trip you wind up feeling like you're working on the conveyor belt called best sights of Venice instead of fully saturating your senses in the
- If you're flying out of Venice pack food for the airport, you'll save $10 on a bad cup of coffee and stale croissant.

Money Mistakes in Venice

Cost	Impact	Solution	Note
Using your home currency	Some credit card rates charge for every transaction in another currency. Check carefully before you use it	Use a prepaid currency card like Wise Multi-Currency Debit Card.	If you wouldn't borrow money from a friend or relative for your trip, don't borrow it from a credit card company.
Renting sunloungers	$20 for two rentals. This cost can take a silent bite out of your budget if you go to Venice's beaches.	Bring a compact beach sofa. Many fit into hand luggage.	
Buying bottled water	At $2 a bottle, this is a cost that can mount up quickly	Refill from the tap. Bring an on the go water filter bottle like Water-to-go.	
Eating like a tourist	Eating at tourist traps can triple your bill. Choose wisely	Star cheap eats on google maps so you're never far from one	
Not agreeing a price of everything in advance	Water taxi's and other unpriced services allow people to con you..	Agree the price beforehand to avoid unwanted bills	
Not getting your VAT refund	22% of all sales purchases	super easy to do at the airport.	'Take your invoice, passport, boarding pass, and goods to the desk of the VAT refund company associated with your store and fill in the tax refund form. The tax refund operator will inform you if you have to go to Customs. Depending on your purchase, you will immediately receive cashback or refund on your credit card.'

The secret to saving HUGE amounts of money when travelling to Venice is…

Your mindset. Money is an emotional topic, if you associate words like cheapskate, Miser (and its £9.50 to go into Charles Dickens Venice house, oh the Irony) with being thrifty when traveling you are likely to say 'F-it' and spend your money needlessly because you associate pain with saving money. You pay now for an immediate reward. Our brains are prehistoric; they focus on surviving day to day. Travel companies and hotels know this and put trillions into making you believe you will be happier when you spend on their products or services. Our poor brains are up against outdated programming and an onslaught of advertisements bombarding us with the message: spending money on travel equals PLEASURE. To correct this carefully lodged propaganda in your frontal cortex, you need to imagine your future self.

Saving money does not make you a cheapskate. It makes you smart. How do people get rich? They invest their money. They don't go out and earn it; they let their money earn more money. So every time you want to spend money, imagine this: while you travel, your money is working for you, not you for money. While you sleep, the money, you've invested is going up and up. That's a pleasure a pricey entrance fee can't give you. Thinking about putting your money to work for you tricks your brain into believing you are not withholding pleasure from yourself, you are saving your money to invest so you can go to even more amazing places. You are thus turning thrifty travel into a pleasure fueled sport.

When you've got money invested - If you want to splash your cash on a first-class airplane seat - you can. I can't tell you how to invest your money, only that you should. Saving $20 on taxis doesn't seem like much, but over time you could save upwards of $15,000 a year, which is a deposit for a house which you can rent on Airbnb to finance more travel. Your brain making money looks like your brain on cocaine, so tell yourself saving money is making money.

Scientists have proved that imagining your future self is the easiest way to associate pleasure with saving money. You can download FaceApp — which will give you a picture of what you will look like older and grayer, or you can take a deep breath just before spending money and ask yourself if you will regret the purchase later.

The easiest ways to waste money traveling are:

Getting a taxi. The solution to this is to always download the google map before you go. Many taxi drivers will drive you around for 15 minutes when the place you were trying to get to is a 5-minute walk... remember while not getting an overpriced taxi to tell yourself, 'I am saving money to free myself for more travel.' Spending money on overpriced food when hungry. The solution: carry snacks. A banana and an apple will cost you, in most places, less than a dollar.

Spending on entrance fees to top-rated attractions. If you really want to do it, spend the money happily. If you're conflicted, sleep on it. I don't regret spending $200 on a sky dive over the Great Barrier Reef; I regret going to the top of the shard on a cloudy day in London for $60. Only you can know, but make sure it's your decision and not the marketing directors at said top-rated attraction.

Telling yourself 'you only have the chance to see/eat/experience it now'. While this might be true, make sure YOU WANT to spend the money. Money spent is money you can't invest, and often you can have the same experience for much less.

You can experience luxurious travel on a small budget, which will trick your brain into thinking you're already a high-roller, which will mean you'll be more likely to act like one and invest your money. Stay in five-star hotels for $5 by booking on the day of your stay on booking.com to enjoy last-minute deals. You can go to fancy restaurants using daily deal sites. Ask your airline about last-minute upgrades to first-class or business. I paid $100 extra on a $179 ticket to Cuba from Germany to be bumped to Business Class. When you ask, it will surprise you what you can get both at hotels and airlines.

Travel, as the saying goes, is the only thing you spend money on that makes you richer. You can easily waste money, making it difficult to enjoy that metaphysical wealth. The biggest money saving secret is to turn bargain hunting into a pleasurable activity, not an annoyance. Budgeting consciously can be fun, don't feel disappointed because you don't spend the $60 to go into an attraction. Feel good because soon that $60 will soon earn money for you. Meaning, you'll have the time and money to enjoy more metaphysical wealth while your bank balance increases.

So there it is. You can save a small fortune by being strategic with your trip planning. We've arranged everything in the guide to offer the best bang for your buck. Which means we took the view that if it's not an excellent investment for your money, we wouldn't include it. Why would a guide called 'Super Cheap' include lots of overpriced attractions? That said, if you think we've missed something or have unanswered questions, ping me an email: philgtang@gmail.com I'm on central Europe time and usually reply within 8 hours of getting your mail. We like to think of our guide books as evolving organisms helping our readers travel better cheaper. We use reader questions via email to update this book year round so you'll be helping other readers and yourself.

Don't put your dreams off!

Time is a currency you never get back and travel is its greatest return on investment. Plus, now you know you can visit Venice for a fraction of the price most would have you believe.

Thank you for reading

Dear **Lovely Reader**,

If you have found this book useful, please consider writing a quick review on Amazon.

One person from every 1000 readers leaves a review on Amazon. It would mean more than you could ever know if you were one of our 1 in 1000 people to take the time to write a brief review.

Thank you so much for reading again and for spending your time and investing your trips future in Super Cheap Insider Guides. One last note, please don't listen to anyone who says 'Oh no, you can't visit Venice on a budget'. Unlike you, they didn't have this book. You can do ANYWHERE on a budget with the right insider advice and planning. Sure, learning to travel to Venice on a budget that doesn't compromise on anything or drastically compromise on safety or comfort levels is a skill, but this guide has done the detective work for you. Now it is time for you to put the advice into action.

Phil and the Super Cheap Insider Guides Team

P.S If you need any more super cheap tips we'd love to hear from you e-mail me at philgtang@gmail.com, we have a lot of contacts in every region, so if there's a specific bargain you're hunting we can help you find it.

DISCOVER YOUR NEXT VACATION

✅ **LUXURY ON A BUDGET APPROACH**
✅ **CHOOSE FROM 107 DESTINATIONS**
✅ **EACH BOOK PACKED WITH REAL-TIME LOCAL TIPS**

All are available in Paperback and e-book on Amazon: https://www.amazon.com/dp/B09C2DHQG5

Several are available as audiobooks. You can watch excerpts of ALL for FREE on YouTube: https://youtube.com/channel/UCxo9YV8-M9P1cFosU-Gjnqg

Super Cheap AUSTRALIA
Super Cheap FRANCE
Super Cheap ICELAND
Super Cheap ITALY
Super Cheap IRELAND
Super Cheap MALDIVES 2023
Super Cheap NORWAY
Super Cheap SWITZERLAND

MORE GUIDES

Super Cheap ADELAIDE 2023
Super Cheap ALASKA 2023
Super Cheap AMSTERDAM 2023
Super Cheap AUSTIN 2023

Super Cheap BANGKOK 2023
Super Cheap BARCELONA 2023
Super Cheap BELFAST 2023
Super Cheap BERMUDA 2023
Super Cheap BORA BORA 2023
Super Cheap Great Barrier Reef 2023
Super Cheap CAMBRIDGE 2023
Super Cheap CANCUN 2023
Super Cheap CHIANG MAI 2023
Super Cheap CHICAGO 2023
Super Cheap DOHA 2023
Super Cheap DUBAI 2023
Super Cheap DUBLIN 2023
Super Cheap EDINBURGH 2023
Super Cheap GALWAY 2023
Super Cheap LAS VEGAS 2023
Super Cheap LIMA 2023
Super Cheap LISBON 2023
Super Cheap MALAGA 2023
Super Cheap Machu Pichu 2023
Super Cheap MIAMI 2023
Super Cheap Milan 2023
Super Cheap NASHVILLE 2023
Super Cheap NEW ORLEANS 2023
Super Cheap NEW YORK 2023
Super Cheap PARIS 2023

Super Cheap SEYCHELLES 2023
Super Cheap SINGAPORE 2023
Super Cheap ST LUCIA 2023
Super Cheap TORONTO 2023
Super Cheap TURKS AND CAICOS 2023
Super Cheap VENICE 2023
Super Cheap VIENNA 2023
Super Cheap YOSEMITE 2023
Super Cheap ZURICH 2023
Super Cheap ZANZIBAR 2023

Bonus Travel Hacks

I've included these bonus travel hacks to help you plan and enjoy your trip to Venice cheaply, joyfully, and smoothly. Perhaps they will even inspire you to start or renew a passion for long-term travel.

Common pitfalls when it comes to allocating money to <u>your desires</u> while traveling

Beware of Malleable mental accounting

Let's say you budgeted spending only $30 per day in Venice but then you say well if I was at home I'd be spending $30 on food as an everyday purchase so you add another $30 to your budget. Don't fall into that trap as the likelihood is you still have expenses at home even if its just the cost of keeping your freezer going.

Beware of impulse purchases in Venice

Restaurants that you haven't researched and just idle into can sometimes turn out to be great, but more often, they turn out to suck, especially if they are near tourist attractions. Make yourself a travel itinerary including where you'll eat breakfast and lunch. Dinner is always more expensive, so the meal best to enjoy at home or as a takeaway. This book is full of incredible cheap eats. All you have to do is plan to go to them.

Social media and FOMO (Fear of Missing Out)

'The pull of seeing acquaintances spend money on travel can often be a more powerful motivator to spend more while traveling than seeing an advertisement.' Beware of what you allow to influence you and go back to the question, what's the best money I can spend today?

Now-or-never sales strategies

One reason tourists are targeted by salespeople is the success of the now-or-never strategy. If you don't spend the money now… your never get the opportunity again. Rarely is this true.

Instead of spending your money on something you might not actually desire, take five minutes. Ask yourself, do I really want this? And return to the answer in five minutes. Your body will either say an absolute yes with a warm, excited feeling or a no with a weak, obscure feeling.

Unexpected costs

"Holding on to anger is like grasping a hot coal with the intent of throwing it at someone else; you only hurt yourself." The Buddha.

One downside to traveling is unexpected costs. When these spring up from airlines, accommodation providers, tours and on and on, they feel like a punch in the gut. During the pandemic my earnings fell to 20% of what they are normally. No one was traveling, no one was buying travel guides. My accountant out of nowhere significantly raised his fee for the year despite the fact there was a lot less money to count. I was so angry I consulted a lawyer who told me you will spend more taking him to court than you will paying his bill. I had to get myself into a good feeling place before I paid his bill, so I googled how to feel good paying someone who has scammed you.

The answer: Write down that you will receive 10 times the amount you are paying from an unexpected source. I did that. Four months later, the accountant wrote to me. He had applied for a COVID subsidy for me and I would receive… you guessed it almost exactly 10 times his fee.

Make of that what you want. I don't wish to get embroiled in a conversation about what many term 'woo-woo', but the result of my writing that I would receive 10 times the amount made me feel much, much better when paying him. And ultimately, that was a gift in itself. So next time some airline or train operator or hotel/ Airbnb sticks you with an unexpected fee, immediately write that you will receive 10 times the amount you are paying from an unexpected source. Rise your vibe and skip the added price of feeling angry.

Hack your allocations for your Venice Trip

"The best trick for saving is to eliminate the decision to save." Perry Wright of Duke University.

Put the money you plan to spend in Venice on a pre-paid card in the local currency. This cuts out two problems - not knowing how much you've spent and totally avoiding expensive currency conversion fees.

You could even create separate spaces. This much for transportation, this for tours/entertainment, accommodation and food. We are reluctant to spend money that is pre-assigned to categories or uses.

Write that you want to enjoy a $3,000 trip for $500 to your Venice trip. Countless research shows when you put goals in writing, you have a higher chance of following through.

Spend all the money you want to on buying experiences in Venice

> **"Experiences are like good relatives that stay for a while and then leave. Objects are like relatives who move in and stay past their welcome." Daniel Gilbert, psychologist from Harvard University.**

Economic and psychological research shows we are happier buying brief experiences on vacation rather than buying stuff to wear so give yourself freedom to spend on experiences knowing that the value you get back is many many times over.

Make saving money a game

There's one day a year where all the thrift shops where me and my family live sell everything there for a $1. My wife and I hold a contest where we take $5 and buy an entire outfit for each other. Whoever's outfit is liked more wins. We also look online to see whose outfit would have cost more to buy new. This year, my wife even snagged me an Armani coat for $1. I liked the coat when she showed it to me, but when I found out it was $500 new; I liked it and wore it a lot more.

Quadruple your money

Every-time you want to spend money, imagine it quadrupled. So the $10 you want to spend is actually $40. Now imagine that what you want to buy is four times the price. Do you still want it? If yes, go enjoy. If not, you've just saved yourself money, know you can choose to invest it in a way that quadruples or allocate it to something you really want to give you a greater return.

Understand what having unlimited amounts of money to spend in Venice actually looks like

Let's look at what it would be like to have unlimited amounts of money to spend on your trip to Venice.

Isolation

You take a private jet to your private Venice hotel. There you are lavished with the best food, drink, and entertainment. Spending vast amounts of money on vacation equals being isolated.

If you're on your honeymoon and you want to be alone with your Amore, this is wonderful, but it can be equally wonderful to make new friends. Know this a study 'carried out by Brigham Young University, Utah found that while obesity increased risk of death by 30%, loneliness increased it by half.'

Comfort

Money can buy you late check outs of five-star hotels and priority boarding on airlines, all of which add up to comfort. But as this book has shown you, saving money in Venice doesn't minimize comfort, that's just a lie travel agencies littered with glossy brochures want you to believe.

You can do late-check outs for free with the right credit cards and priority boarding can be purchased with a lot of airlines from $4. If you want to go big with first-class or business, flights offset your own travel costs by renting your own home or you can upgrade at the airport often for a fraction of what you would have paid booking a business flight online.

MORE TIPS TO FIND CHEAP FLIGHTS

"The use of travelling is to regulate imagination by reality, and instead of thinking how things may be, to see them as they are." Samuel Jackson

If you're working full-time, you can save yourself a lot of money by requesting your time off from work starting in the middle of the week. Tuesdays and Wednesdays are the cheapest days to fly. You can save thousands just by adjusting your time off.

The simplest secret to booking cheap flights is open parameters. Let's say you want to fly from Chicago to Paris. You enter the USA in from and select France under to. You may find flights from New York City to Paris for $70. Then you just need to find a cheap flight to NYC. Make sure you calculate full costs, including if you need airport accommodation and of course getting to and from airports, **but in nearly every instance open parameters will save you at least half the cost of the flight.**

If you're not sure about where you want to go, use open parameters to show you the cheapest destinations from your city. Start with skyscanner.net they include the low-cost airlines that others like Kayak leave out. Google Flights can also show you cheap destinations. To see these leave the WHERE TO section blank.

Open parameters can also show you the cheapest dates to fly. If you're flexible, you can save up to 80% of the flight cost. Always check the weather at your destination before you book. Sometimes a $400 flight will be $20, because it's monsoon season. But hey, if you like the rain, why not?

ALWAYS USE A PRIVATE BROWSER TO BOOK FLIGHTS

Skyscanner and other sites track your IP address and put prices up and down based on what they determine your strength of conviction to buy. e.g. if you've booked one-way and are looking for the return, these sites will jack the prices up by in most cases 50%. Incognito browsing pays.

Use a VPN such as Hola to book your flight from your destination

Install Hola, change your destination to the country you are flying to. The location from which a ticket is booked can affect the price significantly as algorithms consider local buying power.

Choose the right time to buy your ticket.

Choose the right time to buy your ticket, as purchasing tickets on a Sunday has been proven to be cheaper. If you can only book during the week, try to do it on a Tuesday.

Mistake fares

Email alerts from individual carriers are where you can find the best 'mistake fares". This is where a computer error has resulted in an airline offering the wrong fare. In my experience, it's best to sign up to individual carriers email lists, but if you ARE lazy Secret Flying puts together a daily roster of mistake fares. Visit https://www.secretflying.com/errorfare/ to see if there're any errors that can benefit you.

Fly late for cheaper prices

Red-eye flights, the ones that leave later in the day, are typically cheaper and less crowded, so aim to book that flight if possible. You will also get through the airport much quicker at the end of the day. Just make sure there's ground transport available for when you land. You don't want to save $50 on the airfare and spend it on a taxi to your accommodation.

Use this APP for same day flights

If your plans are flexible, use 'Get The Flight Out' (http://www.gtfoflights.com/) a fare tracker Hopper that shows you same-day deeply discounted flights. This is best for long-haul flights with major carriers. You can often find a British Airways round-trip from JFK Airport to Heathrow for $300. If you booked this in advance, you'd pay at least double.

Take an empty water bottle with you

Airport prices on food and drinks are sky high. It disgusts me to see some airports charging $10 for a bottle of water. ALWAYS take an empty water bottle with you. It's relatively unknown, but most airports have drinking water fountains past the security check. Just type in your airport name to wateratairports.com to locate the fountain. Then once you've passed security (because they don't allow you to take 100ml or more of liquids) you can freely refill your bottle with water.

Round-the-World (RTW) Tickets

It is always cheaper to book your flights using a DIY approach. First, you may decide you want to stay longer in one country, and a RTW will charge you a hefty fee for changing your flight. Secondly, it all depends on where and when you travel and as we have discussed, there are many ways to ensure you pay way less than $1,500 for a year of flights. If you're travelling long-haul, the best strategy is to buy a return ticket, say New York, to Bangkok and then take cheap flights or transport around Asia and even to Australia and beyond.

Cut your costs to and from airports

Don't you hate it when getting to and from the airport is more expensive than your flight! And this is true in so many cities, especially European ones. For some reason, Google often shows the most expensive options. Use Omio to compare the cheapest transport options and save on airport transfer costs.

Car sharing instead of taxis

Check if Venice has car sharing at the airport. Often they'll be tons of cars parked at the airport that are half the price of taking a taxi into the city. In most instances, you register your driving licence on an app and scan the code on the car to get going.

Checking Bags

Sometimes you need to check bags. If you do, put an AirTag inside. That way, you'll be about to see when you land where your bag is. This saves you the nail biting wait at baggage claim. And if worse comes to worst, and you see your bag is actually in another city, you can calmly stroll over to customer services and show them where your bag is.

Is it cheaper and more convenient to send your bags ahead?

Before you check your bags, check if it's cheaper to send them ahead of you with sendmybag.com obviously if you're staying in an Airbnb, you'll need to ask the hosts permission or you can time them to arrive the day after you. Hotels are normally very amenable.

What Credit Card Gives The Best Air Miles?

You can slash the cost of flights just for spending on a piece of plastic.

LET'S TALK ABOUT DEBT

Before we go into the best cards for each country, let's first talk about debt. The US system offers the best and biggest rewards. Why? Because they rely on the fact that many people living in the US will not pay their cards in full and the card will earn the bank significant interest payments. Other countries have a very different attitude towards money, debt, and saving than Americans. Thus in Germany and Austria the offerings aren't as favourable as the UK, Spain and Australia, where debt culture is more widely embraced. The takeaway here is this: **Only spend on one of these cards when you have set-up an automatic total monthly balance repayment. Don't let banks profit from your lizard brain!**

The best air-mile credit cards for those living in the UK

Amex Preferred Rewards Gold comes out top for those living in the UK for 2023.

Here are the benefits:

- 20,000-point bonus on £3,000 spend in first three months. These can be used towards flights with British Airways, Virgin Atlantic, Emirates and Etihad, and often

other rewards, such as hotel stays and car hire.
- 1 point per £1 spent
- 1 point = 1 airline point
- Two free visits a year to airport lounges
- No fee in year one, then £140/yr

The downside:

- Fail to repay fully and it's 59.9% rep APR interest, incl fee

You'll need to cancel before the £140/yr fee kicks in year two if you want to avoid it.

The best air-mile credit cards for those living in Canada

Aeroplan is the superior rewards program in Canada. The card has a high earn rate for Aeroplan Points, generating 1.5 points per $1 spent on eligible purchases. Look at the specifics of the eligible purchases https://www.aircanada.com/ca/en/aco/home/aeroplan/earn.html. If you're not spending on these things AMEX's Membership Rewards program offers you the best returns in Canada.

The best air-mile credit cards for those living in Germany

If you have a German bank account, you can apply for a Lufthansa credit card.

Earn 50,000 award miles if you spend $3,000 in purchases and paying the annual fee, both within the first 90 days.

Earn 2 award miles per $1 spent on ticket purchases directly from Miles & More integrated airline partners.

Earn 1 award mile per $1 spent on all other purchases.

The downsides

the €89 annual fee

Limited to fly with Lufthansa and its partners but you can capitalise on perks like the companion pass and airport lounge vouchers.

You need excellent credit to get this card.

The best air-mile credit cards for those living in Austria

"In Austria, Miles & More offers you a special credit card. You get miles for each purchase with the credit card. The Miles & More program calculates miles earned based on the distance flown and booking class. For European flights, the booking class is a flat rate. For intercontinental flights, mileage is calculated by multiplying the booking class by the distance flown." They offer a calculator so you can see how many points you could earn: https://www.miles-and-more.com/at/en/earn/airlines/mileage-calculator.html

The best air-mile credit cards for those living in Spain:

"The American Express card is the best known and oldest to earn miles, thanks to its membership Rewards program. When making payments with this card, points are added, which can then be exchanged for miles from airlines such as Iberia, Air Europa, Emirates or Alitalia." More information is available here: https://www.americanexpress.com/es-es/

The best air-mile credit cards for those living in Australia

ANZ Rewards Black comes out top for 2023.

180,000 bonus ANZ Reward Points (can get an $800 gift card) and $0 annual fee for the first year with the ANZ Rewards Black
Points Per Spend: 1 Velocity point on purchases of up to

$5,000 per statement period and 0.5 Velocity points thereafter.
Annual Fee: $0 in the first year, then $375 after.
Ns no set minimum income required, however, there is a minimum credit limit of $15,000 on this card.

Here are some ways you can hack points onto this card:
https://www.pointhacks.com.au/credit-cards/anz-rewards-black-guide/

The best air-mile credit card solution for those living in the USA with a POOR credit score

The downside to Airline Mile cards is that they require good or excellent credit scores, meaning 690 or higher.

If you have bad credit and want to use credit card air lines you will need to rebuild your credit poor. The Credit One Bank® Platinum Visa® for Rebuilding Credit is a good credit card for people with bad credit who don't want to place a deposit on a secured card. The Credit One Platinum Visa offers a $300 credit limit, rewards, and the potential for credit-limit increases, which in time will help rebuild your score.

PLEASE don't sign-up for any of these cards if you can't trust yourself to repay it in full monthly. This will only lead to stress for you.

Frequent Flyer Memberships

"Points" and "miles" are often used interchangeably, but they're usually two very different things. Maximise and diversify your rewards by utilising both.

A frequent-flyer program (FFP) is a loyalty program offered by an airline. They are designed to encourage airline customers to fly more to accumulate points (also called miles, kilometres, or segments) which can be redeemed for air travel or other rewards.

You can sign up with any FFP program for free. There are three major airline alliances in the world: Oneworld, SkyTeam and Star Alliance. I am with One World https://www.oneworld.com/members because the points can be accrued and used for most flights.

The best return on your points is to use them for international business or first class flights with lie-flat seats. You would need 3 times more miles compared to an economy flight, but if you paid cash, you'd pay 5 - 10 times more than the cost of the economy flight, so it really pays to use your points only for upgrades. The worst value for your miles is to buy an economy seat or worse, a gift from the airlines gift-shop.

Sign up for a family/household account to pool miles together. If you share a common address, you can claim the miles with most airlines. You can use AwardWallet to keep track of your miles. Remember that they only last for 2 years, so use them before they expire.

How to get 70% off a Cruise

An average cruise can set you back $4,000. If you dream of cruising the oceans, but find the pricing too high, look at repositioning cruises. You can save as much as 70% by taking a cruise which takes the boat back to its home port.

These one-way itineraries take place during low cruise seasons when ships have to reposition themselves to locations where there's warmer weather.

To find a repositioning cruise, go to vacationstogo.com/repositioning_cruises.cfm. This simple and often overlooked booking trick is great for avoiding long flights with children and can save you so much money!

It's worth noting we don't have any affiliations with any travel service or provider. The links we suggest are chosen based on our experience of finding the best deals.

Pack like a Pro

"He who would travel happily must travel light." – Antoine de St. Exupery 59.

Travel as lightly as you can. We always need less than we think. You will be very grateful that you have a light pack when changing trains, travelling through the airport, catching a bus, walking to your accommodation, or climbing stairs.

Make a list of what you will wear for 7 days and take only those clothes. You can easily wash your things while you're travelling if you stay in an Airbnb with a washing machine or visit a local laundrette. Roll your clothes for maximum space usage and fewer wrinkles. If you feel really nervous about travelling with such few things, make sure you have a dressier outfit, a little black dress for women is always valuable, a shirt for men. Then pack shorts, a long pair of pants, loose tops and a hoodie to snuggle in. Remind yourself that a lack of clothing options is an opportunity to find bargain new outfits in thrift stores. You can either sell these on eBay after you've worn them or post them home to yourself. You'll feel less stressed, as you don't have to look after or feel weighed down by excess baggage. Here are three things to remember when packing:

- Co-ordinate colours - make sure everything you bring can be worn together.

- Be happy to do laundry - fresh clothes when you're travelling feels very luxurious.

- Take liquid minis no bigger than 60ml. Liquid is heavy, and you simply don't need to carry so much at one time.

- Buy reversible clothes (coats are a great idea), dresses which can be worn multiple different ways.

Checks to Avoid Fees

Always have 6 months' validity on your passport

To enter most countries, you need 6 months from the day you land. Factor in different time zones around the world if your passport is on the edge. Airport security will stop you from boarding your flight at the airport if your passport has 5 months and 29 days left.

Google Your Flight Number before you leave for the airport

Easily find out where your plane is from anywhere. Confirm the status of your flight before you leave for the airport with flightaware.com. This can save you long unnecessary wait times.

Check-in online

The founder, Ryan O'Leary of budget airline Ryanair famously said: "We think they should pay €60 for [failing to check-in online] being so stupid.". Always check-in online, even for international flights. Cheaper international carriers like Scoot will charge you at the airport to check-in.

Checking Bags

Never, ever check a bag if you can avoid it. Sometimes you need to check bags. If you do, put an AirTag inside. That way, you'll be about to see when you land where your bag is. This saves you the nail biting wait at baggage claim. And if worse comes to worst, and you see your bag is actually in another city, you can calmly stroll over to customer services and show them where your bag is.

Is it cheaper and more convenient to send your bags ahead?

Before you check your bags, check if it's cheaper to send them ahead of you with sendmybag.com obviously if you're staying in an Airbnb, you'll need to ask the hosts permission or you can time them to arrive the day after you. Hotels are normally very amenable.

It is always cheaper to put heavier items on a ship, rather than take them on a flight with you. Find the best prices for shipping at https://www.parcelmonkey.com/delivery-services/shipping-heavy-items

Use a fragile sticker

Put a 'Fragile' sticker on anything you check to ensure that it's handled better as it goes through security. It'll also be one of the first bags released after the flight, getting you out of the airport quicker.

If you check your bag, photograph it

Take a photo of your bag before you check it. This will speed up the paperwork if it is damaged or lost.

Relaxing at the Airport

The best way to relax at the airport is in a lounge where they provide free food, drinks, comfortable chairs, luxurious amenities (many have showers) and, if you're lucky, a peaceful ambience. If you're there for a longer time, look for Airport Cubicles, sleep pods which charge by the hour.

You can use your FFP Card (Frequent Flyer Memberships) to get into select lounges for free. Check your eligibility before you pay.

If you're travelling a lot, I'd recommend investing in a Priority Pass for the airport.

It includes 850-plus airport lounges around the world. The cost is $99 for the year and $27 per lounge visit or you can pay $399 for the year all inclusive.

If you need a lounge for a one-off day, you can get a Day Pass. Buy it online for a discount, it always works out cheaper than buying at the airport. Use www.LoungePass.com.

Lounges are also great if you're travelling with kids, as they're normally free for kids and will definitely cost you less than snacks for your little ones. The rule is that kids should be seen and not heard, so consider this before taking an overly excited child who wants to run around, or you might be asked to leave even after you've paid.

Money: How to make it, spend it and save it while travelling

How to earn money WHILE travelling

"Twenty years from now you will be more disappointed by the things you didn't do than by the ones you did do. So throw off the bowlines. Sail away from the safe harbour." - H. Jackson Brown

Digital nomads receive a lot of hype. Put simply, they are " professionals who work online and therefore don't need to tie themselves to one particular office, city, or even country."

The first step in becoming a digital nomad, earning money while travelling, is knowing what you can offer. Your market is the entire world. So, what product or service would you like to offer that they would pay for? Take some time to think about this. In German, they say you should do whatever comes easily to your hand. For example, I've always loved finding bargains, it comes easily to me. Yet I studied Law and Finance at University, which definitely did not come easy. It's not a shock that it didn't transpire into a career. And served more as a lesson in not following my ego.

There are thousands of possibilities to generate income while travelling; offering services like tutorial, coaching, writing service, PR, blogging. Most travellers I meet try their hand at blogging and earning from the advertisements. This is great if you have some savings, but if you need to earn straight away to travel, this should be on the back burner, as it takes time to establish. Still, if this comes easily to you, do it!

You want to make good money fast. Ask yourself, what is it you are good at and how can you deliver maximum value to other people? Here are some ideas if you're totally dumfounded:

1. Teaching English online - you will need a private room for this. Be aware that if you're from the USA and the country you want to work in requires a federal-level background check, it may take months, so apply early. Opportunities are on: t.vipkid.com.cn, abc360.com, italki.com, verbalplanet.com and

verbling.com. You can expect to earn $20 an hour.

1. Work in a hostel. Normally you'll get some cash and free accommodation.
2. Fruit picking. I picked Bananas in Tully, Australia for $20 an hour. The jobs are menial but can be quite meditative. Look on WWOOF.org for organic farm work. There are also amazing opportunities on worldpacker.com and workaway.com
3. fiverr.com - offer a small service, like making a video template and changing the content for each buyer.
4. Do freelance work online: marketing, finance, writing, App creation, graphic designer, UX or UI designer, SEO optimiser / expert. Create a profile on upwork.com - you need to put in a lot of work to make this successful, but if you have a unique skill like coding or marketing, it can be very lucrative.
5. Make a udemy.com course. Can you offer a course in something people will pay for? e.g. stock trading, knitting or marketing.
6. Use Skype to deliver all manner of services: language lessons, therapy, coaching etc. Google for what you could offer. Most specialisms have a plat-

form you can use to find clients and they will take a cut of your earnings/ require a fee.

7. You could work on luxury yachts in the med. It's hard work, but you can save money - Desperate-Sailors.com

8. Become an Airbnb experience host - but this requires you to know one place and stay there for a time. And you will need a work visa for that country.

9. Work on a cruise ship. This isn't a digital nomad job but it will help you travel and save at the same time.

10. Rent your place out on Airbnb while you travel and get a cleaner to manage it. The easiest solution if you own or have a long-term rent contract.

Passive Income Ideas that earn $1000+ a month

- Start a YouTube Channel.
- Start a Membership Website.
- Write a Book.
- Create a Lead Gen Website for Service Businesses.
- Join the Amazon Affiliate Program.
- Market a Niche Affiliate Opportunity.
- Create an Online Course.
- Invest in Real Estate
-

How to spend money

Bank ATM fees vary from $2.50 per transaction to as high as $5 or more, depending on the ATM and the country. You can completely skip those fees by paying with card and using a card which can hold multiple currencies.

Budget travel hacking begins with a strategy to spend without fees. Your individual strategy depends on the country you legally reside in as to what cards are available. Happily there are some fin-tech solutions which can save you thousands on those pesky ATM withdrawal fees and are widely available globally. Here are a selection of cards you can pre-charge with currency for Venice:

N26

N26 is a 12-year-old digital bank. I have been using them for over 6 years. The key advantage is fee-free card transactions abroad. They have a very elegant app, where you can check your timeline for all transactions listed in real time or manage your in-app security anywhere. The card you receive is a Mastercard so you can use it everywhere. If you lose the card, you don't have to call anyone, just open the app and swipe 'lock card'. It puts your purchases into a graph automatically so you can see what you spend on. You can open an account from abroad entirely online, all you need is your passport and a camera n26.com

Revolut

Revolut is a multi-currency account that allows you to hold and exchange 29 currencies and spend fee-free abroad. It's a UK based neobank, but accepts customers from all over the world.

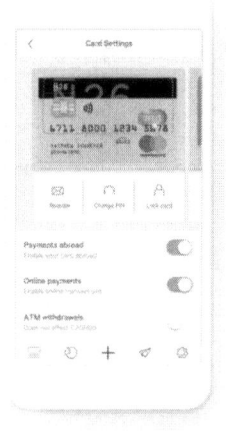

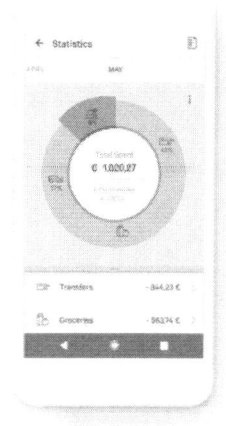

Wise debit card

If you're going to be in one place for a long time, the Wise debit card is like having your travel money on a card – it lets you spend money at the real exchange rate.

Monzo

Monzo is good if your UK based. They offer a fee-free UK account. Fee-free international money transfers and fee-free spending abroad.

The downside

The cards above are debit cards, meaning you need to have money in those accounts to spend it. This comes with one big downside: safety. Credit card issuers' have "zero liability" meaning you're not liable for unauthorised charges. All the cards listed above do provide cover for unauthorised charges but times vary greatly in how quickly you'd get your money back if it were stolen.

The best option is to check in your country to see which credit cards are the best for travelling and set up monthly payments to repay the whole amount so you don't pay unnecessary interest. In the USA, Schwab regularly ranks at the top for travel credit cards. Credit cards are always the safer option when abroad simply because you get your money back faster if its stolen and if you're renting cars, most will give you free insurance when you book the car rental using the card, saving you money.

Always withdraw money; never exchange.

Money exchanges, whether they be on the streets or in the airports will NEVER give you a good exchange rate. Do not bring bundles of cash. Instead, withdraw local currency from the ATM as needed and try to use only free ATMs. Many in airports charge you a fee to withdraw cash. Look for bigger ATMs attached to banks to avoid this.

Recap

- Take cash from local, non-charging ATMs for the best rates.

- Never change at airport exchange desks unless you absolutely have to, then just change just enough to be able get to a bank ATM.

- Bring a spare credit card for emergencies.

- Split cash in various places on your person (pockets, shoes) and in your luggage. It's never sensible to keep your cash or cards all in one place.

- In higher risk areas, use a money belt under your clothes or put $50 in your shoe or bra.

Revolut

Revolut is a multi-currency account that allows you to hold and exchange 29 currencies and spend fee-free abroad. It's a UK based neobank, but accepts customers from all over the world.

Wise debit card
If you're going to be in one place for a long time the Wise debit card is like having your travel money on a card – it lets you spend money at the real exchange rate.

Monzo
Monzo is good if your UK based. They offer a fee-free UK account. Fee-free international money transfers and fee-free spending abroad.

The downside

The cards above are debit cards, meaning you need to have money in those accounts to spend it. This comes with one big downside: safety. Credit card issuers' have "zero liability" meaning you're not liable for unauthorised charges. All of the cards listed above do provide cover for unauthorised charges but times vary greatly in how quickly you'd get your money back if it were stolen.

The best option is to check in your country to see which credit cards are the best for travelling and set up monthly payments to repay the whole amount so you don't pay unnecessary interest. In the USA, Schwab[2] regularly ranks at the top for travel credit cards. Credit cards are always the safer option when abroad simply because you get your money back faster if its stolen and if you're renting cars, most will give you free insurance when you book the car rental using the card, saving you money.

---

[2] Charles Schwab High Yield Checking accounts refund every single ATM fee worldwide, require no minimum balance and have no monthly fee.

Always withdraw money; never exchange.

Money exchanges whether they be on the streets or in the airports will NEVER give you a good exchange rate. Do not bring bundles of cash. Instead withdraw local currency from the ATM as needed and try to use only free ATM's. Many in airports charge you a fee to withdraw cash. Look for bigger ATM's attached to banks to avoid this.

Recap

- Take cash from local, non-charging ATMs for the best rates.
- Never change at airport exchange desks unless you absolutely have to, then just change just enough to be able get to a bank ATM.
- Bring a spare credit card for emergencies.
- Split cash in various places on your person (pockets, shoes) and in your luggage. Its never sensible to keep your cash or cards all in one place.
- In higher risk areas, use a money belt under your clothes or put $50 in your shoe or bra.

How to save money while travelling

Saving money while travelling sounds like an oxymoron, but it can be done with little to no effort. Einstein is credited as saying, "Compound interest is the eighth wonder of the world." If you saved and invested $100 today, in 20 years, it would be $2,000 thanks to the power of compound interest. It makes sense then to save your money, invest and make even more money.

The Acorns app is a simple system for this. It rounds up your credit card purchases and puts the rest into a savings account. So if you pay for a coffee and its $3.01, you'll save 0.99 cents. You won't even notice you're saving by using this app: www.acorns.com

Here are some more generic ways you can always save money while travelling:

Device Safety

Having your phone, iPad or laptop stolen is one BIG and annoying way you can lose money travelling. The simple solution is to use apps to track your devices. Some OSes have this feature built-in. Prey will try your smartphones or laptops (preyproject.com).

Book New Airbnb's

When you take a risk on a new Airbnb listing, you save money. Just make sure the hosts profile is at least 3 years old and has reviews.

If you end up in an overcrowded city

The website https://campspace.com/ is like Airbnb for camping in people's garden and is a great way to save money if you end up in a city during a big event.

Look out for free classes

Lots of hostels offer free classes for guests. If you're planning to stay in a hostel, check out what classes your hostel offers. I have learnt languages, cooking techniques, dance styles, drawing and all manner of things for free by taking advantage of free classes at hostels.

Get student discounts

If you're studying buy an ISIC card - International Student Identity Card. It is internationally recognised, valid in 133 countries and offers more than 150,000 discounts!

Get Senior Citizen discounts

Most state run attractions, ie, museums, galleries will offer a discount for people over 65 with ID.

Instal maps.me

Maps me is extremely good for travelling without data. It's like offline google maps without the huge download size.

Always buy travel insurance

Don't travel without travel insurance. It is a small cost to pay compared with what could be a huge medical bill.

Travel Apps That'll Make Budget Travel Easier

Travel apps are useful for booking and managing travel logistics. They have one fatal downside: they can track you in the app and keep prices up. If you face this, access the site from an incognito browser tab.

Here are the best apps and what they can do for you:

- Best For flight Fare-Watching: Hopper.

- Best for booking flights: Skyscanner and Google Flights

- Best for timing airport arrivals: FlightAware - check on delays, cancellations and gate changes.

- Best for overcoming a fear of flying: SkyGuru - turbulence forecasts for the route you're flying.

- Best for sharing your location: TripWhistle - text or send your GPS coordinates or location easily.

- Best for splitting expenses among co-travellers: Splittr, Trip Splitter, Venmo or Splitwise.

How NOT to be ripped off

"One of the great things about travel is that you find out how many good, kind people there are."
— Edith Wharton

The quote above may seem ill placed in a chapter entitled how not to be ripped off, but I included it to remind you that the vast majority of people do not want to rip you off. In fact, scammers are normally limited to three situations:

1. Around heavily visited attractions - these places are targeted purposively due to sheer footfall. Many criminals believe ripping people off is simply a numbers game.

2. In cities or countries with low-salaries or communist ideologies. If they can't make money in the country, they seek to scam foreigners. If you have travelled to India, Morocco or Cuba you will have observed this phenomenon.

3. When you are stuck and the person helping you know you have limited options.

Scammers know that most people will avoid confrontation. Don't feel bad about utterly ignoring someone and saying no. Here are six strategies to avoid being ripped off:

1. **Never ever agree to pay as much as you want. Always decide on a price before.**

Whoever you're dealing with is trained to tell you, they are uninterested in money. This is a trap. If you let people do this they will ask for MUCH MORE money at the end, and because you have used there service, you will feel obliged to pay. This is a conman's trick and nothing more.

2. Pack light

You can move faster and easier. If you take heavy luggage, you will end up taking taxis which are comparatively very costly over time.

3. NEVER use the airport taxi service. Plan to use public transport before you reach the airport.

4. Don't buy a sim card from the airport. Buy from the local supermarkets it will cost 50% less.

5. Eat at local restaurants serving regional food

Food defines culture. Exploring all delights available to the palate doesn't need to cost enormous sums.

6. Ask the locals what something should cost, and try not to pay over that.

7. If you find yourself with limited options. e.g. your taxi dumps you on the side of the road because you refuse to pay more (common in India and parts of South America) don't act desperate and negotiate as if you have other options or you will be extorted.

8. Don't blindly rely on social media[3]

Let's say you post in a Facebook group that you want tips for travelling to The Maldives. A lot of the comments you will receive come from guides, hosts and restaurants doing their own promotion. It's estimated that 50% or more of

---

[3] https://arstechnica.com/tech-policy/2019/12/social-media-platforms-leave-95-of-reported-fake-accounts-up-study-finds/

Facebook's current monthly active users are fake. And what's worse, a recent study found Social media platforms leave 95% of reported fake accounts up. These accounts are the digital versions of the men who hang around the Grand Palace in Bangkok telling tourists its closed, to divert you to shops where they will receive a commission for bringing you.

It can also be the case that genuine comments come from people who have totally different interests, beliefs and yes, budgets to yours. Make your experience your own and don't believe every comment you read.

Bottom line: use caution when accepting recommendations on social media and always fact-check with your own research.

Small tweaks on the road add up to big differences in your bank balance

Take advantage of other hotel amenities

If you fancy a swim but you're nowhere near the ocean, try the nearest hotel with a pool. As long as you buy a drink, the hotel staff will probably grant you access.

Fill up your mini bar for free.

Fill up your mini bar for free by storing things from the breakfast bar or grocery shop in your mini bar to give you a greater selection of drinks and food without the hefty price tag.

Save yourself some ironing

Use the steam from the shower to get rid of wrinkles in clothing. If something is creased, leave it trapped with the steam in the bathroom overnight for even better results.

See somewhere else for free

Opt for long stopovers, allowing you to experience another city without spending much money.

Wear your heaviest clothes

On the plane to save weight in your pack, allowing you to bring more with you. Big coats can then be used as pillows to make your flight more comfortable.

Don't get lost while you're away.

Find where you want to go using Google Maps, then type 'OK Maps' into the search bar to store this information for offline viewing.

Use car renting services

Share Now or Car2Go allow you to hire a car for 2 hours for $25 in a lot of European countries.

Share Rides

Use sites like blablacar.com to find others who are driving in your direction. It can be 80% cheaper than normal transport. Just check the drivers reviews.

Use free gym passes

Get a free gym day pass by googling the name of a local gym and free day pass.

When asked by people providing you a service where you are from..

If there's no price list for the service you are asking for, when asked where you are from, Say you are from a lesser-known poorer country. I normally say Macedonia, and if they don't know where it is, add it's a poor country. If you say UK, USA, the majority of Europe bar the well-known poorer countries taxi drivers, tour operators etc will match the price to what they think you pay at home.

Set-up a New Uber/ other car hailing app account for discounts

By googling you can find offers with $50 free for new users in most cities for Uber/ Lyft/ Bolt and alike. Just set up a new gmail.com email account to take advantage.

Where and How to Make Friends

"People don't take trips, trips take people." – John Steinbeck

Become popular at the airport

Want to become popular at the airport? Pack a power bar with multiple outlets and just see how many friends you can make. It's amazing how many people forget their chargers, or who packed them in the luggage that they checked in.

Stay in Hostels

First of all, Hostels don't have to be shared dorms, and they cater to a much wider demographic than is assumed. Hostels are a better environment for meeting people than hotels, and more importantly, they tended to open up excursion opportunities that further opened up that opportunity.

Or take up a hobby

If hostels are a definite no-no for you; find an interest. Take up a hobby where you will meet people. I've dived for years and the nature of diving is you're always paired up with a dive buddy. I met a lot of interesting people that way.

Small tweaks on the road add up to big differences in your bank balance

Take advantage of other hotel's amenities

If you fancy a swim but you're nowhere near the ocean, try the nearest hotel with a pool. As long as you buy a drink, the hotel staff will likely grant you access.

Fill up your mini bar for free.

Fill up your mini bar for free by storing things from the breakfast bar or grocery shop in your mini bar to give you a greater selection of drinks and food without the hefty price tag.

Save yourself some ironing

Use the steam from the shower to get rid of wrinkles in clothing. If something is creased, leave it trapped with the steam in the bathroom overnight for even better results.

See somewhere else for free

Opt for long stopovers, allowing you to experience another city without spending much money.

Wear your heaviest clothes

on the plane to save weight in your pack, allowing you to bring more with you. Big coats can then be used as pillows to make your flight more comfortable.

Don't get lost while you're away.

Find where you want to go using Google Maps, then type 'OK Maps' into the search bar to store this information for offline viewing.

Use car renting services

Share Now or Car2Go allow you to hire a car for 2 hours for $25 in a lot of Europe.

Share Rides

Use sites like blablacar.com to find others who are driving in your direction. It can be 80% cheaper than normal transport. Just check the drivers reviews.

Use free gym passes

Get a free gym day pass by googling the name of a local gym and free day pass.

When asked by people providing you a service where you are from..

If there's no price list for the service you are asking for, when asked where you are from, Say you are from a lesser-known poorer country. I normally say Macedonia, and if they don't know where it is, add it's a poor country. If you say UK, USA, the majority of Europe bar the well-known poorer countries taxi drivers, tour operators etc will match the price to what they think you pay at home.

Set-up a New Uber/ other car hailing app account for discounts

By googling you can find offers with $50 free for new users in most cities for Uber/ Lyft/ Bolt and alike. Just set up a new gmail.com email account to take advantage.

Where and How to Make Friends

"People don't take trips, trips take people." – John Steinbeck

Become popular at the airport

Want to become popular at the airport? Pack a power bar with multiple outlets and just see how many friends you can make. It's amazing how many people forget their chargers, or who packed them in the luggage that they checked in.

Stay in Hostels

First of all, Hostels don't have to be shared dorms, and they cater to a much wider demographic than is assumed. Hostels are a better environment for meeting people than hotels, and more importantly they tended to open up excursion opportunities that further opened up that opportunity.

Or take up a hobby

If hostels are a definite no-no for you; find an interest. Take up a hobby where you will meet people. I've dived for years and the nature of diving is you're always paired up with a dive buddy. I met a lot of interesting people that way.

When unpleasantries come your way...

We all have our good and bad days travelling, and on a bad day you can feel like just taking a flight home. Here are some ways to overcome common travel problems:

Anxiety when flying

It has been over 40 years since a plane has been brought down by turbulence. Repeat that number to yourself: 40 years! Planes are built to withstand lighting strikes, extreme storms and ultimately can adjust course to get out of their way. Landing and take-off are when the most accidents happen, but you have statistically three times the chance of winning a huge jackpot lottery, then you do of dying in a plane crash.

If you feel afraid on the flight, focus on your breathing saying the word 'smooth' over and over until the flight is smooth. Always check the airline safety record on <u>airlinerating.com</u> I was surprised to learn Ryanair and Easyjet as much less safe than Wizz Air according to those ratings because they sell similarly priced flights. If there is extreme turbulence, I feel much better knowing I'm in a 7 star safety plane.

Wanting to sleep instead of seeing new places

This is a common problem. Just relax, there's little point doing fun things when you feel tired. Factor in jet-lag to your travel plans. When you're rested and alert you'll enjoy your new temporary home much more. Many people hate the first week of a long-trip because of jet-lag and often blame this on their first destination, but its rarely true. Ask travellers who 'hate' a particular place and you will see that very often they either had jet-lag or an unpleasant journey there.

Going over budget

Come back from a trip to a monster credit card bill? Hopefully, this guide has prevented you from returning to an unwanted bill. Of course, there are costs that can creep up and this is a reminder about how to prevent them making their way on to your credit card bill:

- To and from the airport. Solution: leave adequate time and take the cheapest method - book before.

- Baggage. Solution: take hand luggage and post things you might need to yourself.

- Eating out. Solution: go to cheap eats places and suggest those to friends.

- Parking. Solution: use apps to find free parking

- Tipping. Solution Leave a modest tip and tell the server you will write them a nice review.

- Souvenirs. Solution: fridge magnets only.

- Giving to the poor. (This one still gets me, but if you're giving away $10 a day - it adds up) Solution: volunteer your time instead and recognise that in tourist destinations many beggars are run by organised crime gangs.

Price v Comfort

I love traveling. I don't love struggling. I like decent accommodation, being able to eat properly and see places and enjoy. I am never in the mood for low-cost airlines or crappy transfers, so here's what I do to save money.

- Avoid organised tours unless you are going to a place where safety is a real issue. They are expensive and constrain your wanderlust to typical things. I only recommend them in Algeria, Iran and Papua New Guinea - where language and gender views pose serious problems all cured by a reputable tour organiser.

- Eat what the locals do.

- Cook in your Airbnb/ hostel where restaurants are expensive.

- Shop at local markets.

- Spend time choosing your flight, and check the operator on arilineratings.com

- Mix up hostels and Airbnbs. Hostels for meeting people, Airbnb for relaxing and feeling 'at home'.

Not knowing where free toilets are

Use Toilet Finder - https://play.google.com/store/apps/details?id=com.bto.toilet&hl=en

Your Airbnb is awful

Airbnb customer service is notoriously bad. Help yourself out. Try to sort things out with the host, but if you can't, take photos of everything e.g bed, bathroom, mess, doors, contact them within 24 hours. Tell them you had to leave and pay for new accommodation. Ask politely for a full refund including booking fees. With photographic evidence and your new accommodation receipt, they can't refuse.

The airline loses your bag

Go to the Luggage desk before leaving the airport and report the bag missing. Hopefully you've headed the advice to put an AirTag in your checked bag and you can show them where to find your bag. Most airlines will give you an overnight bag, ask where you're staying and return the bag to you within three days. It's extremely rare for Airlines to lose your bag due to technological innovation, but if that happens you should submit an insurance claim after the three days is up, including receipts for everything you had to buy in the interim.

Your travel companion lets you down

Whether it's a breakup or a friend cancelling, it sucks and can ramp up costs. The easiest solution to finding a new travel companion is to go to a well-reviewed hostel and find someone you want to travel with. You should spend at least three days getting to know this person before you suggest travelling together. Finding someone in person is always better than finding someone online, because you can get a better idea of whether you will have a smooth journey together. Travel can make or break friendships.

Culture shock

I had one of the strongest culture shocks while spending 6 months in Japan. It was overwhelming how much I had to prepare when I went outside of the door (googling words and sentences what to use, where to go, which station and train line to use, what is this food called in Japanese and how does its look etc.). I was so tired constantly but in the end I just let go and went with my extremely bad Japanese. If you feel culture shocked its because your brain is referencing your surroundings to what you know. Stop comparing, have Google translate downloaded and relax.

Your Car rental insurance is crazy expensive

I always use carrentals.com and book with a credit card. Most credit cards will give you free insurance for the car, so you don't need to pay the extra. Some unsavoury companies will bump the price up when you arrive. Ask to speak to a manager. If this doesn't resolve, it google "consumer ombudsman for NAME OF COUNTRY." and seek an immediate full refund on the balance difference you paid. It is illegal in most countries to alter the price of a rental car when the person arrives to pickup a pre-arranged car.

A note on Car Rental Insurance

Always always always rent a car with a credit card that has rental vehicle coverage built into the card and is automatically applied when you rent a car. Then there's no need to buy additional rental insurance (check with your card on the coverage they protect some exclude collision coverage). Do yourself a favour when you step up to the desk to rent the car tell the agent you're already covered and won't be buying anything today. They work on commission and you'll save time and your patience avoiding the upselling.

You're sick

First off ALWAYS, purchase travel insurance. Including emergency transport up to $500k even to back home, which is usually less than $10 additional. I use https://www.comparethemarket.com/travel-insurance/ to find the best days. If I am sick I normally check into a hotel with room service and ride it out.

Make a Medication Travel Kit

Take travel sized medications with you:

- Antidiarrheal medication (for example, bismuth subsalicylate, loperamide)

- Medicine for pain or fever (such as acetaminophen, aspirin, or ibuprofen)

- Throat Lozenges

Save yourself from most travel related hassles

- Do not make jokes with immigration and customs staff. A misunderstanding can lead to HUGE fines.

- Book the most direct flight you can find nonstop if possible.

- Carry a US$50 bill for emergency cash. I have entered a country and all ATM and credit card systems were down. US$ can be exchanged nearly anywhere in the world and is useful in extreme situations, but where possible don't exchange, as you will lose money.

- Check, and recheck, required visas and such BEFORE the day of your trip. Some countries, for instance, require a ticket out of the country in order to enter. Others, like the US and Australia, require electronic authorisation in advance.

- Airport security is asinine and inconsistent around the world. Keep this in mind when connecting flights. Always leave at least 2 hours for international connections or international to domestic. In Stansted for example, they force you to buy one of their plastic bags, and remove your liquids from your own plastic bag.... just to make money from you. And this adds to the time it will take to get through security, so lines are long.

- Wiki travel is perfect to use for a lay of the land.

- Expensive luggage rarely lasts longer than cheap luggage, in my experience. Fancy leather bags are toast with air travel.

Food

- When it comes to food, eat in local restaurants, not tourist-geared joints. Any place with the menu in three or more languages is going to be overpriced.

- Take a spork - a knife, spoon and fork all in one.

Water Bottle

Take a water bottle with a filter. We love these ones from Water to Go.

Empty it before airport security and separate the bottle and filter as some airport people will try and claim it has liquids…

Bug Sprays

If you're heading somewhere tropical spray your clothes with Permethrin before you travel. It lasts 40 washes and saves space in your bag. A 'Bite Away' zapper can be used after the bite to totally erase it. It cuts down on the itching and erases the bite from your skin.

Order free mini's

Don't buy those expensive travel sized toiletries, order travel sized freebies online. This gives you the opportunity to try brands you've never used before, and who knows, you might even find your new favourite soap.

Take a waterproof bag

If you're travelling alone you can swim without worrying about your phone, wallet and passport laying on the beach.

You can also use it as a source of entertainment on those ultra budget flights.

Make a private entertainment centre anywhere

Always take an eye-mask, earplugs, a scarf and a kindle reader - so you can sleep and entertain yourself anywhere!

The best Travel Gadgets

The door alarm

If you're nervous and staying in private rooms or airbnbs take a door alarm. For those times when you just don't feel safe, it can help you fall asleep. You can get tiny ones for less than $10 from Amazon: https://www.amazon.com/Travel-door-alarm/s?k=Travel+door+alarm

Smart Blanket

Amazon sells a 6 in 1 heating blanket that is very useful for cold plane or bus trips. Its great if you have poor circulation as it becomes a detachable Foot Warmer: Amazon http://amzn.to/2hTYlOP I paid $49.00.

The coat that becomes a tent

https://www.adiff.com/products/tent-jacket. This is great if you're going to be doing a lot of camping.

Clever Tank Top with Secret Pockets

Keep your valuables safe in this top. Perfect for all climates.

on Amazon for $39.90

Optical Camera Lens for Smartphones and Tablets

Leave your bulky camera at home. Turn your device into a high-performance camera. Buy on Amazon for $9.95

Travel-sized Wireless Router with USB Media Storage

Convert any wired network to a wireless network. Buy on Amazon for $17.99.

Buy a Scrubba Bag to wash your clothes on the go

Or a cheaper imitable. You can wash your clothes on the go.

Hacks for Families

Rent an Airbnb apartment so you can cook

Apartments are much better for families, as you have all the amenities you'd have at home. They are normally cheaper per person too. We are the first travel guide publisher to include Airbnb's in our recommendations if you think any of these need updating you can email me at philgtang@gmail.com

Shop at local markets

Eat seasonal products and local products. Get closer to the local market and observe the prices and the offer. What you can find more easily, will be the cheapest.

Take Free Tours

Download free podcast tours of the destination you are visiting. The podcast will tell you where to start, where to go, and what to look for. Often you can find multiple podcast tours of the same place. Listen to all of them if you like, each one will tell you a little something new.

Pack Extra Ear Phones

If you go on a museum tour, they often have audio guides. Instead of having to rent one for each person, take some extra earphones. Most audio tour devices have a place to plug in a second set.

Buy Souvenirs Ahead of Time

If you are buying souvenirs somewhere touristy, you are paying a premium price. By ordering the same exact products online, you can save a lot of money.

Use Cheap Transportation

Do as the locals do, including weekly passes.

Carry Reusable Water Bottles

Spending money on water and other beverages can quickly add up. Instead of paying for drinks, take some refillable water bottles.

Combine Attractions

Many major cities offer ticket bundles where one price gets you into 5 or 6 popular attractions. You will need to plan ahead of time to decide what things you plan to do on vacation and see if they are selling these activities together.

Pack Snacks

Granola bars, apples, baby carrots, bananas, cheese crackers, juice boxes, pretzels, fruit snacks, apple sauce, grapes, and veggie chips.

Stick to Carry-On Bags

Do not pay to check a large bag. Even a small child can pull a carry-on.

Visit free art galleries and museums

Just google the name + free days.

Eat Street Food

There's a lot of unnecessary fear around this. You can watch the food prepared. Go for the stands that have a steady queue.

Travel Gadgets for Families

Dropcam

Are what-if scenarios playing out in your head? Then you need Dropcam.

'Dropcam HD Internet Wi-Fi Video Monitoring Cameras help you watch what you love from anywhere. In less than a minute, you'll have it setup and securely streaming video to you over your home Wi-Fi. Watch what you love while away with Dropcam HD.'

Approximate Price: $139

Kelty-Child-Carrier

Voted as one of the best hiking essentials if you're traveling with kids and can carry a child up to 18kg.

Jetkids Bedbox

No more giving up your own personal space on the plane with this suitcase that becomes a bed.

Safety

"If you think adventure is dangerous, try routine. It's lethal." – Paulo Coelho

Backpacker murdered is a media headline that leads people to think traveling is more dangerous than it is. The media sensationalise the rare murders and deaths of backpackers and travellers. The actual chances of you dying abroad are extremely extremely low.

Let's take the USA as an example. In 2018, 724 Americans **died** from unnatural causes, 167 died from car accidents, while the majority of the other deaths resulted from drownings, suicides, and non-vehicular accidents. Contrast this with the 15,000 murders in the US in 2018, and travelling abroad looks much safer than staying at home.

There are many things you can to keep yourself safe. Here are our tips.

1. Always check fco.co.uk before travelling. NEVER RELY on websites or books. Things are changing constantly and the FCO's (UK's foreign office) advice is always UP TO DATE (hourly) and **extremely conservative**.

2. Check your mindset. I've travelled alone to over 180 countries and the main thing I learnt is if you walk around scared, or anticipating you're going to be pickpocketed, your constant fear will attract bad energy. Murders or attacks on travellers are the mainstay of media, not reality, especially in countries familiar with travellers. The only place I had cause to genuinely fear for my life was Papua New Guinea -

where nothing actually happened to me only my own panic over culture shock.

There are many things you can do to stop yourself being victim to the two main problems when travelling: theft or being scammed.

I will address theft first. Here are my top tips:

- Stay alert while you're out and always have an exit strategy.

- Keep your money in a few different places on your person and your passport somewhere it can't be grabbed.

- Take a photo of your passport on your phone in case. If you do lose it, google for your embassy, you can usually get a temporary pretty fast.

- Google safety tips for travelling in your country to help yourself out and memorise the emergency number.

- At hostels, keep your large bag in the room far under the bed/out of the way with a lock on the zipper.

- On buses/trains, I would even lock my bag to the luggage rack.

- Get a personal keychain alarm. The sound will scare anyone away.

- Don't wear any jewellery. A man attempted to rob a friend of her engagement ring in Bogota, Colombia, and in hindsight I wished I'd told her to leave it at home/wear it on a hidden necklace, as the chaos it created was avoidable.

- Don't turn your back to traffic while you use your phone.

- When travelling in the tuktuk sit in the middle and keep your bag secure. Wear sunglasses as dust can easily get in your eyes.

- Don't let anyone give you flowers, bracelets, or any type of trinket, even if they insist it's for free and compliment you like crazy.

- Don't let strangers know that you are alone - unless they are travel friends ;-)

- Lastly, and most importantly -Trust your gut! If it doesn't feel right, it isn't.

How I got hooked on budget travelling

'We're on holiday' is what my dad used to say to justify getting us in so much debt we lost our home and all our things when I was 11. We moved from the suburban bliss of Hemel Hempstead to a run down council estate in inner-city London, near my dad's new job as a refuge collector, a fancy word for dustbin man. I lost all my school friends while watching my dad go through a nervous breakdown.

My dad loved walking up a hotel lobby desk without a care in the world. So much so, that he booked overpriced holidays on credit cards. A lot of holidays. As it turned out, we couldn't afford any of them. In the end, my dad had no choice but to declare bankruptcy. When my mum realised, he'd racked up so much debt our family unit dissolved. A neat and perhaps as painless a summary of events that lead me to my life's passion: budget travel that doesn't compromise on fun, safety or comfort.

I started travelling full-time at the age of 18. I wrote the first Super Cheap Insider guide for friends visiting Norway - which I did for a month on less than $250. When sales reached 10,000 I decided to form the Super Cheap Insider Guides company. As I know from first-hand experience debt can be a noose around our necks, and saying 'oh come on, we're on vacation' isn't a get out of jail free card. In fact, its the reverse of what travel is supposed to bring you - freedom.

Before I embarked upon writing Super Cheap Insider guides, many, many people told me that my dream was impossible. Travelling on a budget could never be comfortable. I hope this guide has proved to you what I have known for a long-time: budget travel can feel luxurious when you know and use the insider hacks.

And apologies if I depressed you with my tale of woe. My dad is now happily remarried and works as a chef in London at a fancy hotel - the kind he used to take us to!

A final word...

There's a simple system you can use to think about budget travel. In life, we can choose two of the following: cheap, fast, or quality. So if you want it Cheap and fast you will get a lower quality service. Fast-food is the perfect example. The system holds true for purchasing anything while travelling. I always choose cheap and quality, except at times where I am really limited on time. Normally, you can make small tweaks to make this work for you. Ultimately, you must make choices about what's most important to you and heed your heart's desires.

'Your heart is the most powerful muscle in your body. Do what it says.' Jen Sincero

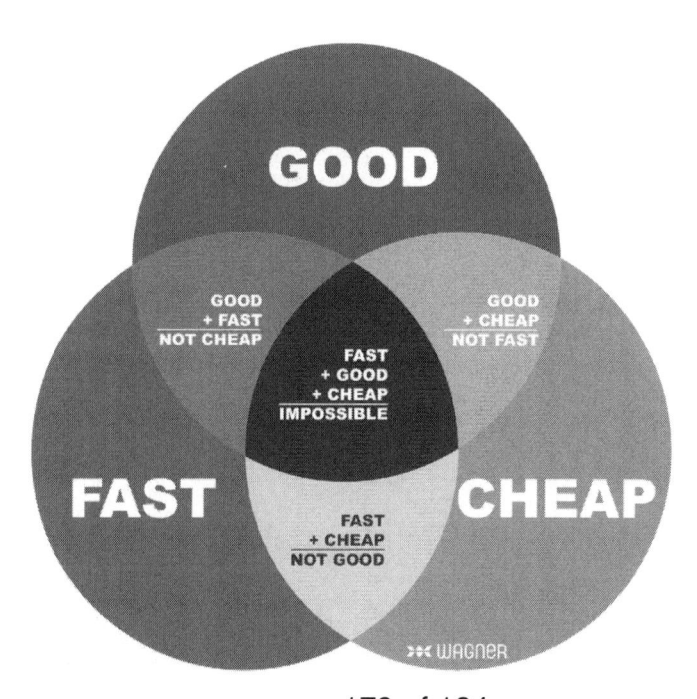

Our Writers

Phil Tang was born in London to Irish immigrant, Phil graduated from The London School of Economics with a degree in Law. Now he travels full-time in search of travel bargains with his wife, dog and a baby and a toddler.

Ali Blythe has been writing about amazing places for 17 years. He loves travel and especially tiny budgets equalling big adventures nearly as much as his family. He recently trekked the Satopanth Glacier trekking through those ways from where no one else would trek. Ali is an adventurer by nature and bargainist by religion.

Michele Whitter writes about languages and travel. What separates her from other travel writers is her will to explain complex topics in a no-nonsense, straightforward way. She doesn't promise the world. But always delivers step-by-step methods you can immediately implement to travel on a budget.

Lizzy McBraith, Lizzy's input on Super Cheap Insider Guides show you how to stretch your money further so you can travel cheaper, smarter, and with more wanderlust. She loves going over land on horses and helps us refine each guide to keep them effective. **If you've found this book useful, please consider leaving a short review on Amazon. it would mean a lot.Copyright**

If you've found this book useful, please select five stars on Amazon. Knowing I helped you plan your trip to Venice would mean genuinely make my day.

Copyright

Published in Great Britain in 2023 by Super Cheap Insider Guides LTD.

Copyright © 2023 Super Cheap Insider Guides LTD.

The right of Phil G A Tang to be identified as the Author of the Work has been asserted in accordance with the Copyright, Designs and Patents Act 1988.

All rights reserved.

No part of this publication may be reproduced, stored in a retrieval system, or transmitted, in any form or by any means without the prior written permission of the publisher, nor be otherwise circulated in any form of binding or cover other than that in which it is published and without a similar condition being imposed on the subsequent purchaser.

All rights reserved. No part of this publication may be reproduced, distributed, or transmitted in any form or by any means, including photocopying, recording, or other electronic or mechanical methods, without the prior written permission of the publisher, except in the case of brief quotations embodied in critical reviews and certain other non-commercial uses permitted by copyright law.

Redefining Super Cheap	10
How to Enjoy ALLOCATING Money in Venice	20
How to feel RICH in Venice	23
Priceline Hack to get a Luxury Hotel on the Cheap	30
Hotels with frequent last-minute booking discounts:	31
Cheapest Guesthouses in Venice	37
How to use this book	48
OUR SUPER CHEAP TIPS…	49
How to Find Super Cheap Flights to Venice	49
How to Find CHEAP FIRST-CLASS Flights to Venice	53
Go Book Shopping	87
RECAP: How to enjoy a $5,000 trip to Venice for $300	100
Money Mistakes in Venice	105
The secret to saving HUGE amounts of money when travelling to Venice is…	106
Thank you for reading	110
Bonus Travel Hacks	114
Common pitfalls when it comes to allocating money to your desires while traveling	115
Hack your allocations for your Venice Trip	118
MORE TIPS TO FIND CHEAP FLIGHTS	121

What Credit Card Gives The Best Air Miles?	126
Frequent Flyer Memberships	130
How to get 70% off a Cruise	132
Pack like a Pro	133
Relaxing at the Airport	136
Money: How to make it, spend it and save it while travelling	138
How to earn money WHILE travelling	139
How to spend money	142
How to save money while travelling	147
Travel Apps That'll Make Budget Travel Easier	148
How NOT to be ripped off	150
Small tweaks on the road add up to big differences in your bank balance	156
Where and How to Make Friends	159
When unpleasantries come your way…	160
Hacks for Families	171
Safety	174
How I got hooked on budget travelling	177
A final word…	179
Our Writers	180
Copyright	182

Printed in Great Britain
by Amazon